MW00906851

Comfort Ye My People:
The Church's Mandate toward Israel and the Jewish People

Dr. Martha J. Smith

WestBow
PRESS
A DIVISION OF THOMAS NELSON

WestBow Press books may be ordered through booksellers or by contacting:

WestBow Press
A Division of Thomas Nelson
1663 Liberty Drive
Bloomington, IN 47403
www.westbowpress.com
1-(866) 928-1240

Because of the dynamic nature of the Internet, any web addresses or links contained in this book may have changed since publication and may no longer be valid. The views expressed in this work are solely those of the author and do not necessarily reflect the views of the publisher, and the publisher hereby disclaims any responsibility for them.

Any people depicted in stock imagery provided by Thinkstock are models, and such images are being used for illustrative purposes only.

Certain stock imagery © Thinkstock.

ISBN: 978-1-4497-5864-6 (sc)
ISBN: 978-1-4497-5863-9 (hc)
ISBN: 978-1-4497-6015-1 (e)

Library of Congress Control Number: 2012912600

Printed in the United States of America

WestBow Press rev. date: 10/24/2012

CONTENTS

FOREWORD

by Ardoine Clauzel, Attorney at Law
Co-director: Étoile du Matin Ministries,
St. Étienne Vallée Francais, France.

If I had to describe this book in a few words, I would say "a must read." This is the "definitive" book which should be read in the times in which we live to be fully aware, as the Church and as citizens, of what's happening behind the scenes. To determine how we must position ourselves appropriately, a strategic biblical perspective based on the facts surrounding Israel is a necessity. Jesus said that "the children of this age are shrewder than are the children of light." (Luke 16-8). This is unfortunately true in many cases, as "the children of light" have frequently acted against their own best interests, in agreeing with those whose only intention is to destroy them. When the Church forgets where it has come from and joins forces with those who oppose Israel, whether passively or actively, it cuts off the branch on which it rests. Many Christians have forgotten their history. If they understood their roots, they would find a pattern that those who persecuted the Jews were later systematically destroying Christians - that is, Christians who were empowered by a living, Biblical faith.

The Roman Empire which cruelly persecuted the Jews, later slaughtered the Christians. The Church of Rome, after having severed its Jewish roots, repeated the pattern of Rome and persecuted the Jews.

They then went on to persecute the other so-called "heretics", such as the Waldensians and the Huguenots, who were actively bringing men and women back to the Gospel and to Biblical faith. History shows that where Jews are persecuted, the believing Church will be sooner or later subjected to the same suffering.

In this book, Martha Smith dismantles the mechanisms that support anti-Semitism to reveal their deep, hidden roots, and to demonstrate that the same logic governing attacks against God's chosen people, the Jews, is used against those who authentically know Jesus, the Jewish Messiah.

A particularly well-supported treatise, while remaining simple and easily understood by all, this book confronts and highlights international political strategies from media sources, their challenges and implications for Israel and for us as Christians. Our fates are clearly linked, whether we wish to admit it or not. We Christians have been grafted into the root of the tree of Israel (Rom. 11.17). So if the trunk is cut, what will become of the branches?! (Rom. 11.18)

As a practicing lawyer in France, I must be extremely attentive to evidence. One of the strengths of this book is that it is based on solid evidence: eyewitness accounts, archival documents and news. As a descendant of the Huguenots and a grand-daughter of leaders in the Belgian Resistance who hid Jews in their home during World War II, I am deeply committed to respect for human rights and the right to freedom of thought and expression for which my ancestors died. This legacy makes me particularly sensitive to the sectarian and anything that can insidiously enforce control over one's right to freedom of thought and speech, no matter what the justification may be.

In a very relevant and substantiated way, Martha Smith denounces today's "political correctness" as an elaborate means of undermining the fundamental freedoms for which our forefathers fought, paying the price for our freedom with their lives. The Church must not allow itself to be deceived by the rhetoric of political correctness. It should be prepared to confront the half-truths and manipulations with the facts regarding Israel. Martha Smith poses, with finesse and acuity, the essential questions for each of us as individuals and as members of the Body of Christ, to position ourselves, but also to accurately assess where we stand today. The Church should have correctly responded to these questions in 1939. We cannot rewrite the past. The future is a blank page.

Biblical prophecies concerning Israel and the Church will come to completion and will be fulfilled without fail. However, based on our response and choices, we can, ourselves, choose a course that would be pleasing to the Lord on that day when our lives will be evaluated by the righteous Judge, the Lord , who Himself is called "the God of Israel" EX. 5-1, 34-23.

ACKNOWLEDGMENTS

To the memory of the more than six million Jews who perished in the Shoa and the brave Resistance who sought to save them and to end the tyranny.
With gratitude to my dear husband, Haakon, the board of IVOJ: Janet, Valerie, Drennan and Don—and to Paul Harmon for his excellent editorial feedback and Penny Drexel for listening to the reading of the book.

Previous Works

Hanna's Treasure Box

Musical: *The Good Sami* (music and text)

Opera: *Beethoven's Fidelio: A Holocaust Memorial*
(production design and text)
(prospectus design–Haakon Smith)

Musical: *The Lamb* (music and text: Martha Smith)

Musical Drama: *Voices of the Holocaust* (text: Martha
Smith; music: Marilee Eckert and Martha Smith)

Musical Drama: *Voices of the Resistance,* (Text: Martha Smith)

Musical: *Steinrøsa, An Alf Prøysen Review*
(Text: Martha Smith; music, Alf Prøysen)

Dissertation: *A Historical and Analytical Guide to the
Anthems of George Friedrich Handel* (Copyright: Martha
J. Smith, Dissertation Abstracts Intl., 1987)

INTRODUCTION

Since the schism of the church from its Jewish roots, anti-Semitic attitudes have pervaded the body of Christ. The blood-libel accusations of the Medieval Ages, the Spanish Inquisition, and the slaughter of Jews throughout "Christian" Europe for centuries have been indicative of the hatred of the Jewish people which was fostered in the church.

One day, during my time of prayer and meditation, the Lord revealed to me, "There is a continual strategizing meeting in hell to see how its forces can attack and take down Israel and the Jews. Satan envies and hates the covenant relationship between the Jewish people and God. God formed an eternal covenant with Abraham, then Isaac and at last with Jacob (whose name was changed to Israel), promising them the land which is now Israel as an eternal possession. He also promised that the Messiah, the savior of the world would come from their lineage, Thus, God established a plan to destroy Satan's kingdom forever through His promises to the Jewish people. Satan is aware of this and has great fury against the Jewish people as a result. He realizes that his days are numbered. In addition, Satan would have for himself all power, blessings, position and honor. Consequently, he despises the fact that mankind has come into a covenant relationship with God through faith in Jesus, the Jewish Messiah, descended from a Jewish king and born of a Jewish virgin.

This diabolical conference has been going on for millennia. The results have been clearly manifest from the time of the patriarchs to the present: the enslavement of the Jews under Pharaoh; Balak's attempts to curse the Hebrews through Balaam; the attack on Abraham and Sara's faith that led to the birth of Ishmael, contributing to the current conflict with the Arab world; the sieges against Israel by Babylon, Persia, Assyria, and Rome in the ancient world; the Spanish Inquisition, centuries of pogroms throughout Europe; the Holocaust; the Yom Kippur War, the Six-Day War, and the first and second intifadas.

In the two thousand years since the Jewish people fled Israel and became a Diaspora, scattered throughout the nations, hell's strategy has manifest itself in the form of constant discrimination and pogroms. Jews were forbidden by law to enter or live in Christian England and Norway for centuries. In the name of Christianity,. Spain and Portugal, two countries having large populations of Jews during the middle ages, inflicted continual pogroms on their Jewish population. At last the horrors of the Inquisition were implemented in both nations which brought about a blood bath and drove the remaining Jews out of these countries. The Jewish inhabitants of the ghettoes of Christian Rome and other Italian cities experienced repeated pogroms and oppressive restrictions.

The Holocaust throughout Christian Europe during World War II was not the first genocide experienced by the Jews of Germany and Austria. In recent excavations in Vienna, a synagogue was found several meters underground with the remains of more than a hundred Jews and their rabbi. They had committed suicide in the fourteen hundreds rather than be burned alive by Gentiles surrounding the synagogue who insisted that the Jews convert to Christianity. Christian Eastern Europe—Poland, Estonia, Latvia, Lithuania, Ukraine, Russia, Bulgaria, Hungary, and Romania—has seen countless pogroms over the centuries. The main justification for these pogroms was the accusation against the Jewish victims: "Christ killers!"

No less threatening for innocent Jewish people was the blood libel, the rumor that Jews would kill Christian children and mix their blood with the flour used to make Passover matzo. This lie, spread by Christians and the church, caused the deaths of countless innocent

Jewish people throughout Europe over the centuries. All of this was done in the name of Christ!

Christians talk about "witnessing to Jewish people," and yes, we are called to be witnesses for Jesus. But Jews cannot hear our words for the suffering that has been afflicted on them over the centuries by Christians in the name of Christ. This is an indictment against the church.

Since the reestablishment of the nation of Israel in 1948, Christians worldwide have begun to awaken and realize the important position the Jewish people have as God's chosen people and timepiece. With this awakening, Christians have begun to declare their unity with Israel and the Jews. The importance of this people and nation in God's eternal plan has become evident.

Let us be challenged as the Gentile body of Jesus, the Messiah, to rid our hearts of all anti-Semitism and indifference toward Israel and the Jewish people. It is time that the church make amends for centuries of persecution of the Jews in the name of Christ. As we approach Israel and her people in a spirit of love and unity, we may see the strongholds of anti-Semitism in our churches, communities, and nations begin to fall. Judgment starts with the house of God, and change must begin with the church—especially since the church has been the main purveyor of anti-Semitism over the centuries.

We, the church of Jesus Christ, must understand that there is no middle ground. We are either for the Jewish people and Israel or against them. During the Holocaust in Europe, Christians were silent as Jewish shops were looted, Jewish homes were ransacked, and innocent Jewish people were transported to concentration camps. Silence means complicity. We can be silent no more. But to speak out, we must have knowledge.

CHAPTER I

The Bennett Avenue Survivors: A Lesson in Love

**Nazi officials with Church Leaders
giving the "Heil Hitler" salute**

"Forgive us for our silence in your time of suffering.
In cattle cars you rolled by, in our churches we did sing.
Forgive us that we did not help when you needed us the most.
Rise up, Christians, for Israel; stand like a mighty host.
—From Corrie Ten Boom's song, *Voices of the Holocaust* [1]

When I was a little girl growing up on a farm in Ohio, my parents bought one of the first televisions in our area. I was fascinated by the music and dance programs. But the images printed indelibly on my memory came from documentary films showing the liberation of German concentration camps. Seeing the dead and the faces of starving people, even as a little child, I had a longing to have done something to help these suffering people.

As I grew older, I heard stories of wars being fought in Israel: the miraculous victories possible only through divine intervention, such as the Six-Day War and the Yom Kippur War. At the age of ten, I met a woman named Esther Turkeltaub who had been an officer in the Israeli army. I was captivated as Esther spoke about Israel and her time in the military. That evening when we returned home, I told my mother, "I would never carry a gun for any country except Israel." My mother laughed, but I think she knew I meant what I said.

When I moved to New York City and settled in the Washington Heights area of northern Manhattan, I discovered that Russian, German, Yiddish, and Hebrew were as common as English on the streets of my new neighborhood. The Lord had placed me in an area inhabited by many European Jewish survivors and refugees, newly arrived Russian Jews, and Israelis. Many Holocaust survivors had resettled there after the war.

On Bennett Avenue, a street that is only twelve blocks long, there were two yeshivas or Jewish religious schools. One was for boys and one for girls. Next to the girls' yeshiva was the Breuer Shul, a synagogue settled by German immigrants. Its first rabbi was Joseph Breuer, who had come from Frankfurt to New York in 1939, fleeing Hitler. A congregation of Orthodox German Jews formed on this street. Bennett Avenue also was home to a lovely Jewish center and a building that housed a recreation and feeding program for elderly Jews. Many refugees who had survived concentration camps were given their hot meal for the day in this center.

On the other side of my building, on Nagle Avenue, was the Young Hebrew Association. The YHA also had a feeding program for the elderly, also mostly Holocaust survivors. Ten blocks away was Yeshiva

University, a major Jewish theological school. Orthodox families would stroll together down Bennett Avenue on Shabbat and the Jewish holidays. In the springtime, the little children from the yeshivas would pass by our apartment building at Purim. It was a delight to see the girls dressed as Esther and the little boys as Mordechai or some other figure. In the fall, I would walk down the street and see booths with branches and leaves on balconies at the Jewish center. Observant families walked by on their way to the booths, carrying food in picnic baskets as they celebrated the Feast of Tabernacles.

At the time, I didn't realize how privileged I was to live in this neighborhood. I was grateful to have an apartment of my own in New York City, where it is so difficult to find affordable accommodations. But as the years passed, I came to understand that God had His hand on my life and had put me right where He needed me to be to prepare me, and eventually my husband, for the work He wanted us to do.

As I opened the door one day at Ehmer's Meats on 181st Street, near Broadway, the employees were speaking German. I had just returned from Austria where I had studied at the Mozarteum Conservatory of Music. I greeted the workers in German. The shop manager, speaking in German, told one of the employees an anti-Semitic joke. (I didn't realize it until a minute later, but I was being tested.)Fortunately, I interjected with righteous indignation, "How can you say such a thing in this neighborhood, filled with Holocaust survivors?" The manager smiled at my response. He introduced himself to me as Chaim. He and his wife Eva then told me of their years as prisoners in Auschwitz. I stood in the middle of the shop listening with tears running down my face as the workers swept and scrubbed the floors around me. I returned many times after this to buy meat at the store, and became friends with all the workers.

One evening, returning home to my apartment from work, I saw Herbert, an Ehmer's employee, speaking German with a group of elderly people sitting on benches and lawn chairs. I said hello to him, and we began to converse. The others seemed wary of me, but as time passed we spent many more evenings together, and they began to trust me. I had worked in synagogues as a professional singer, and I often sang

Hebrew songs for them on these summer evenings in the rose garden. They were Jews who had come out of Hitler's inferno. They seemed eager to talk about their suffering, and I spent many hours listening. Their plight became a pivotal force in my life. Eventually, my dear friends on Bennett Avenue allowed me to collect their stories on tape. I intended to compile them into a book, but instead they became the material for a musical drama called *Voices of the Holocaust* that has since been performed in concert in many nations of Europe.

My friends in the rose garden were from many different backgrounds: Doris Shafran was from Czechoslovakia. Sofie Aron came from Turkey, and her husband, Alfred, was from Hamburg, Germany. Herbert Lichtenstein was from Oberwesel am Rhein, Germany, and his wife, Ursala (Ushie) Cohen Lichtenstein, was from Berlin. Rose Cohen Constan and her daughter Marion and son Guy were also from Berlin. Armin Friedman was from Riga, Latvia, and Bernard Gombins was from Poland. They had been in concentration camps and then refugee camps before coming to New York. I saw the numbers that had been tattooed on their arms when they entered the camps. They spoke of their mothers, fathers, sisters, brothers, grandparents, aunts, uncles, and friends who had been forced into the same camp-bound trains as they were. They never saw their loved ones again. They had perished in the gas chambers.

My survivor friends told me of unspeakable horrors they had seen in the camps: hangings, death marches, people being shot for stealing scraps of bread, women being ripped apart and their unborn children being killed on the end of a bayonet. They spoke of prisoners who, unable to take the torment anymore, ran into an electric fence to die, their bodies shaking with its high-voltage charge while guards riddled them with bullets. For nine years, Haakon and I lived in their midst, loving them, weeping and laughing with them, celebrating birthdays with them, singing and playing for their Zionist organizations to raise money for Israel. They became our *mishpochah*—our family. We began to realize that their friendship and trust was a gift from God and that we had been given a divine mandate to carry their stories to the world..

I felt honored that they would share their hearts with me and allow me to collect their stories. (Stephen Spielberg later sent a film crew to this neighborhood and recorded the stories of many of my dear friends. These films are now in the archives of the US Holocaust Memorial Museum in Washington, D.C.)

Our friends, the Bennett Avenue survivors, had a profound influence on us, and their stories have served as a springboard for this book and our other work. Over the years, in pondering the tragedy and horror through which they lived, many questions have often crossed my mind:

What if the Christians of Europe hadn't been silent?

What if they had spoken out in the beginning, when Hitler's followers were still few?

What if the church, as a whole, had stood up against Hitler and denounced his plans?

What if the church hadn't been a participant over many centuries in pogroms against Jews throughout Europe?

And what if Martin Luther hadn't written anti-Semitic diatribes?

What if? Would the Holocaust still have happened? Could an outspoken church have prevented this genocide? Would there have been the massive numbers of dead, or would the loss of life have been minimal if believers in Jesus had taken a stand? Some may say it's senseless to ask such questions. Done is done; past is past. But I think it is required of Christians to ask these questions. Would Hitler have taken power at all if the church had stood against him in the initial stages of his ascent? Very few Christians at that time would risk their lives to help Jews. Most remained silent. Would we—this generation of believers—have done differently if we had been there?

We all need to ask ourselves: What would Jesus have done? And what would I have done if I had been there? Perhaps one can never know for certain the answer to that question. But we can ask what we must do today to prevent such a thing from happening again.

We must learn the lessons of history if we are to avoid the pitfalls of the past in our generation. The best history teachers I know are my dear friends, the Bennett Avenue survivors, and I will let them speak for themselves. The following are the monologues and poems from *Voices of the Holocaust*,[1] a work which has been performed in many nations of Europe.

> Where, oh where are my children?
> You have stolen them from me.
> The long years pass and the memories of pain fade away.
> But the children, the children are not.
> Rachel weeps for the child that is not.
> But Ushie weeps for the child that never was.
> —From Ushie's song, *Voices of the Holocaust*

Photo by: M. Smith

Ushie Lichtenstein

Ushie's story

It was not easy for Ushie Lichtenstein, Herbert's widow, to talk in her later years, because of Parkinson's disease. But it was always difficult for Ushie to talk about what had happened to her in the camps.

Because Ushie's family name was Cohen, her father, Saul, would carry the Torah in their synagogue, as was the custom for the Cohenim.

6

Saul was a kind man. When he came home from their clothing shop in Berlin, he would often bring Ushie and her sisters, Ruth and Laila, presents. But a day came when their papa didn't return home. The SS general Reinhard Heydrich had been assassinated in Prague. In retaliation, 500 Jewish men in Berlin were rounded up and executed at Lichtenfeld airfield. Saul Cohen was one of them.

Then Ushie, her mother, and Laila were taken to Theresienstadt. Ruth was sent to Auschwitz with her husband. Ushie, Laila and their mother first worked in a factory, assembling weapons. Ushie was eventually placed in the kitchen where she prepared soup made from rotten vegetables. One day Ushie fell while carrying a large pot of hot water. She nearly died from third-degree burns over much of her body.

But there were secrets she found hard to share. One day Ushie called and asked me to come to her home. She wanted to talk and it seemed urgent. I arrived as quickly as I could. Ushie had an almost wild look in her eyes.

She had always said that she couldn't have children because of the effects of starvation. But on that day Ushie revealed the real reason for her barreness. She had been abused by guards and soldiers at Theresienstadt. When she became pregnant, she was force-sterilized. Ushie was only fifteen at the time.

> The Rhine valley is a quiet place to grow up,
> the son of a kosher butcher. The Lorelei
> stares down from her precipice, concealing the
> secret knowledge of what is to come for
> the boy in the valley. Like evil magic, she spins a
> web of deception, entangling the minds
> of the people. A madness, hysteria, insanity. That
> blood should flow o'er the streets of
> the land like the waters of the Rhine flowing to
> the sea. No, it could not happen in this
> little town near the Lorelei. It's such a quiet place.
> Herbert Lichtenstein's Song from *Voices of the Holocaust*

Photo by: M. Smith

Herbert Lichtenstein

Herbert's story

"I remember Krystal Nacht well. I was living in Berlin at the time, working as an apprentice to a kosher butcher. I would follow in my father's footsteps and take over the family butcher shop in Oberwesel am Rhein.

"I had traveled home many times on this train from Berlin to Rheinland. But there was something strange about this trip. In every station where we stopped, the platforms were filled with Jewish people. Some were with families; some stood alone. Some had suitcases; some were covered with blood. All seemed to have a look of horror on their faces. I learned from a Jewish passenger on the train that across the nation, synagogues and Jewish shops were being destroyed and Jews were fleeing for their lives. I stayed on the train for three days and nights, not knowing where to go or what to do. The night skies were lit with the flames of burning buildings as I traveled back and forth across the country.

"After this, it was clear that we Jews must leave Germany. But how? Our assets were frozen or stolen, our businesses closed. Most of us could no longer finance an escape. I entered a program to prepare for emigration to Palestine, financed by the Jewish agency. I would learn to be a farmer. But before my papers were processed and I could book passage, I was taken in transport as a slave laborer. I was first sent to Bielefeld where I worked with a team of prisoners cutting down a forest area where we would build a munitions factory. Then I was sent to Buchenwald. One day, the barracks to which I was assigned was evacuated. I managed to slip away with three other prisoners. We hid in the garbage dump. All of the others from our barracks were taken to the gas chambers that day and killed. My next destination was Auschwitz, where I was assigned to work in the Yavishuwitz coal mine. I worked in freezing temperatures with very little clothing. On Sundays, our free day, the guards at Auschwitz would arrange "sport" for us. We were ordered to march in circles for hours. The emaciated prisoners dropped in exhaustion, one after the other. Those of us left standing were ordered to march on top of the bodies of the fallen or we would be shot and killed.

"Finally, I was sent to Theresienstadt. It was there I first met Ushie, my future wife. We were not sweethearts until some years later when we met at a dance for refugees in New York City. But in Theresienstadt, we worked together in the kitchen. There was no thought of romance or marriage. It was survival, one bite of food at a time, one hour at a time. *Arbeit macht frei* (Work makes freedom). But where was the freedom? The only freedom to be found in this hell we were living in was the freedom of death. But how could it happen in Germany? This was the land of Goethe, Schiller, Beethoven, the greatest minds of our time. How?"

Haakon and I spent many a Friday night (Shabbos) with Herbert and Ushie. One Friday evening, I asked Herbert how he felt when he visited the Western Wall in Jerusalem for the first time. For the first and only time in all the years I had known him, Herbert began to cry and said, "That was the greatest moment of my life, greater than the end of the war and being released from the camp." He said he felt he had come home.

On another Shabbos, Herbert looked at us and said, "You are the children we could never have." In 1997, Herbert was dying of kidney failure from a beating he had received at Auschwitz. The guards had discovered a newspaper in Herbert's shoes which reported that the Germans were losing on the eastern front. They beat Herbert so severely in the kidney area that he had blood in his urine for more than a month. As he lay dying, Herbert said, "There is a bank account in Oberwesel am Rhein that I want you to have. Every month my grandfather had put money in the account for Mette (Herbert's sister, who died at Auschwitz) and me. It isn't a lot of money, but I want to get a lawyer who can arrange for you and Haakon to have that money." Herbert died before he could do so. But the fact that he and Ushie had wanted us to have an inheritance from them was a gift beyond words.

Photo: by permission of Yad Vashem

Aboard the St. Louis

That we should live when they should die, it is a
mystery, a quiet, haunting guilt, that the
passing decades cannot, cannot erase, but only
intensifies, recalling to memory the faces
of the lost. The mothers, the fathers, the children,
the doctors, professors, artists, rabbis,
the wealthy, and those whose every possession
was sold to make the fateful, hopeless
journey. Their images never dissipate, recurring
in the quiet recesses of sleep. Bursting
before their eyes in moments meant to be times
of joy. But only to be submerged in the
tank of pain that remembrance brings. The millions
sacrificed to pagan demon gods cry,
cry from the funeral pyres that evoke and demand
our remembrance. This is our duty.
This is why we lived when they died.
—From The Arons and the St. Louis - Song *Voices of the Holocaust*

Sofi and Alfred Aron's story

"Mazeltov! La Chaim! Alfred and I stood under the *chupah*, the wedding canopy. He was so handsome as his foot crashed down upon the glass. There had been much shattered glass of late in Hamburg. It was five months after Krystal Nacht. As they carried Alfred and me on chairs above the crowd of well-wishers after the wedding ceremony, I couldn't help but think about the ship that would soon carry us on our honeymoon. What a strange place for a Turkish-Jewish woman and a German-Jewish man to go for their honeymoon—Havana, Cuba. We left Germany on May 13, 1939. We were sharing this journey with nearly a thousand Jews, eager to start a new life of freedom.

"The ship was quite elegant, and one would never know that the passengers were fleeing for their lives. But the Gestapo had gone before us and bribed the Cubans to reject our legal entrance visas. Only a handful of those on board who already had relatives living in Cuba managed to disembark. The rest of us sailed in circles between the coast of Florida and Cuba, seeking asylum in the Americas. The compassionate captain, Gustav Schroeder, radioed different governments in the Americas to request visas for the passengers. But the answer was always the same. No one would receive us; no one wanted us.

"Finally, we returned to Europe, sailing to Antwerp. Alfred was taken to Dachau. I was protected by the Turkish consul. I managed to buy Alfred out of Dachau, providing we would leave Germany immediately. We returned to Cuba, this time gaining entry. But from the nearly one thousand passengers on the ship, very few survived. Why were we spared?"

> Mother, mother, I see you. I'm reaching out to
> grasp you. Come closer, Mother. Don't
> let them take you away. Are you there? No, it was only a dream.
> —From Doris Shaffran's song, *Voices of the Holocaust*

Photo by: M. Smith

Doris Shaffran

Doris Shafran's story

"We never dreamed the Germans would come to Prague. They said they only wanted Sudetenland. It was German. It had been agreed. But suddenly they were everywhere in their stiff uniforms, with their guns with bayonets. We were forced to wear an arm band with the Magen David, the star of David. Gentile neighbors, once our friends, shunned, ridiculed, and betrayed us.

"Finally, we were forced into transport trains going east. Mother and I were able to stay together. We had lost contact with the rest of the family as we were pressed tightly into the cattle cars. Starting, stopping, the doors never opening, the thirst burning in our throats ... standing in defecation ... the dead dropping around us, impossible to move with so many people jammed into so small a space. Three days passed and we arrived at our destination. The doors swung open. Barking dogs, bright lights, shouting soldiers, bayonets glistening.

"Where were we? Hell itself, it seemed. They called it Auschwitz. Inspection lines, the old, the weak, the sick, small children—all to the left. To the left, woman, the girl to the right.

"'Mother, I am going with you.'

"'No, my child. Do what the man says. I am old and have lived my life. You are young, and you deserve a chance.'

"'I am going with you, Mother.'

"'To the right, girl!' the soldier shouted, and he shoved me.

"'Mother!'"

Photo: by: M. Smith

Rose Cohen Constan

13

Photo: by: M. Smith

Marion Constan Sylvester

A mother would give all of her jewels and gold,
even her own life, to know her children
live and are well. A mother would give all.
—From Rose Cohen Constan's song, *Voices of the Holocaust*

Out of the eyes of a child into the blackness of
night: the barbed wire fences, the barking
of dogs, the gaunt, void faces of prisoners, the
meaningless hours spent in lines as
numbers pour forth through the air. A child
with no name, only a number.
—From Marian Constan Sylvester's song, *Voices of the Holocaust*

Rose and Marion Constan's story

"Why should it cost so much to hide four Jews—my husband, Leopold, and my children, Marian and Guy, and myself? But they wanted more and more, these so-called French patriots. They pretended to care about us, but all they really cared about was our money.

Finally, there was nothing left but the jewels from my mother, my inheritance. They were hard to give up, not because of their monetary value, but because they represented the glory my family had once had. Father, the government minister, the war hero, decorated by the Kaiser. The grand soirees in our mansion in Berlin. The jewels were the last link to the past. But to these 'patriots' I wasn't the daughter of the Kaiser's close associate and minister. I wasn't even human. I was just another Jew trying to buy her life and the lives of her family with diamonds and gold. At last everything was gone. We were sold by our French 'protectors' to the Gestapo. I wonder what they got for turning us in. Were we as valuable as the gems, mere pieces of rock, which I had sold to buy our lives?

"Marion and I were sent to one side of the concentration camp. Leopold was on the men's side. Guy fled to the woods. He was caught by Vichy vigilantes and gathered together with a hundred Jews in a schoolhouse where all were shot. Because Guy was small, the bullets missed him. He lay under the bodies of the victims while the murderers made sure there were no survivors. When they left to get trucks to take away the bodies, Guy fled to the countryside. He met a French family who hid him until the war ended.

"After the war, we found each other again through the rabbi in the village outside of Paris where we had been in hiding before being sold to the Gestapo. What a joy it was when we discovered that all the family had survived.

"It may seem strange, but I now know that I haven't lost my heritage. Oh, yes, the jewels are gone. But my children are my inheritance, and they live.

Haakon and I spent much time with Rose and Marion. Rose lived in an apartment on the floor above us. Marion lived on the same floor as Herbert and Ushie in another building. I saw Rose quite frequently when we went to our post boxes to get the mail. When I asked how she was, her response was: Alvaz gut! or "Always good." She lived to the ripe age of 102.

There were so many other survivors and refugees who touched our lives in Washington Heights. I would be remiss if I did not honor them as well.

Bernard Gombins was a neighbor from a nearby building who had fled from his native Poland to Russia and survived the war. But all of his family in Poland perished in the death camps. Bernard called himself a free-thinker. He said that he wasn't a "religious man" but that he came from a religious family. In spite of the tragedy he had experienced, Bernard had a ready smile and a joyous, sincere laugh. However, there was always an underlying sadness in his eyes.

Suzie, a friend of Herbert and Ushie, who lived on the floor above them, had resettled in New York before the war. She was from Turkey. Suzie kindly gave of herself and spent time teaching me the Ladino text for a song I was learning for a concert. (Ladino is the Spanish dialect spoken by the Sephardic Jews who had fled the Inquisition and settled around the nations of the Mediterranean, Turkey included.)

Ruth Löwenstein, who also lived in Herbert and Ushie's building, had come to New York from Germany before the war. She was a nurse. After retirement, Ruth did volunteer work among the survivors in the Washington Heights area.

Rachmiel Frydland

Torn between two worlds, the God of our fathers and the God I found. *Sh'ma Israel Adonai Elohenu, Adonai echad.* But the mystery is one.
—From Rachmiel Frydland's song, *Voices of the Holocaust*

Perhaps the greatest influence on my life among the survivors I have known is Rachmiel Frydland. He was born in Chelm, Poland, and educated as a Hassidic rabbi. All the members of his family were killed during the Holocaust. Rachmiel survived the Warsaw Ghetto and Auschwitz through his faith in Yeshua-Jesus, the Messiah.

When I was going through a particularly difficult time in my life, someone gave me a copy of Rachmiel's testimony. His courage and faith in the Lord gave me strength to keep going. I read and reread the little testimony booklet many times.

Later I met him at a messianic synagogue in New York City. When Rachmiel visited New York, he often attended the church where I was working as director of music. Out of love, Rachmiel preached the Gospel on the streets of New York. Once he had come late to a meeting because he had to return to his residence to change clothes—his suit had been covered with spit.

Arrival at Auschwitz, Photo by permission of Yad Vashem

Arrival at Auschwitz Birkenau, Photo by permission of Yad Vashem

Siegen Synagogue ablaze on Krystal Nacht Nov. 1938
Photo by permission of Yad Vashem

Warsaw Ghetto Arrest, Photo by permission of Yad Vashem

Sometimes God's greatest blessings are not silver and gold, but friendships. Haakon and I spent many Friday nights with Herbert and Ushie in their apartment, listening as they described their teenage years growing up in Nazi Germany and their fight for survival in the camps. We were honored when Herbert and Ushie declared us to be the children they could never have. They commissioned us to take their stories to the world. That is what we have endeavored to do through the work of International Voice of Justice. IVOJ is a nonprofit established to produce arts events for Holocaust education throughout the world with a special concentration on European countries.

We must not forget the more than six million Jews who died in the time of Jacob's trouble, the Holocaust. Even as the first song of *Voices of the Holocaust* reminds us:

Photo: Elie Wiesel Foundation

Cry it, shout it, proclaim it to the world. They must remember and not forget. Every life of the six million shall not be in vain. Eli! Eli! Lama sabachthani? My God, my God, why have you forsaken us, your people? Remember them. Remember them. Remember them.

—Elie Wiesel's cry

1. Smith. Martha: Voices of the Holocaust, a musical drama: Text: Martha Smith, Music: Marilee Eckert and Martha Smith. Copyright: 1994, Library of Congress

CHAPTER 2

But That Was a Long Time Ago

Many Christians may ask, "The Holocaust took place a long time ago. Why do we need to be so aware of it today?" George Santayana warned, "Those who cannot remember the past are condemned to repeat it." The world is forgetting.

Anti-Semitic attitudes did not disappear with the end of World War II. In 2010, traveling by train from Oswiecim, the Polish town where the Auschwitz and Birkenau camps had been, to Krakow, I saw suspicious graffiti painted on the walls of stations where the train stopped. I wrote down the text and took it to our Polish business partners in Krakow to ask them if the text was anti-Semitic. Their reply was: "Decidedly so."

Hatred of Jews has not ended. It is therefore important for us, as Christians called to stand with God's chosen people, to keep abreast of societal attitudes toward the Jewish people and Israel.

The International Herald Tribune of January 25, 2012, carried an article entitled "Study shows persistence of anti-Semitic attitudes."[1] The study, commissioned by the German parliament, revealed that 20 percent of Germans still harbor hatred for Jews. The research further revealed that anti-Semitic attitudes have grown in countries such as Poland, Hungary, and Portugal, with growth to a lesser degree in Italy, Britain, the Netherlands, and France. The survey showed that one-fifth of Germans agreed with stereotypical anti-Semitic statements.

On June 12, 2011, Norway's leading newspaper ran a report with the headline "Hatred of Jews in Oslo Schools."[2] a survey conducted by Oslo city commissioners revealed that one in three Jewish children ages fourteen to sixteen had been attacked by anti-Semitic speech or physical bullying in city schools, three to five times a month. The poll also revealed that *Jew* was regularly used by school children as a negative word to demean other students.

Across the world, anti-Semitic attacks have grown in number:

France: From September 29 to November 6, 2000, ninety-three synagogues were defaced or set on fire, according to Israeli Ambassador to Norway, Amos Nadai.

Caracas, Venezuela: In February 2009, the Jewish community center was attacked by a fire bomb. One month earlier, a synagogue was desecrated in the city.

Berlin, Germany: In February 2007, a smoke bomb was thrown into a Jewish kindergarten but failed to ignite.

Mombai, India: On Nov. 28, 2008, terrorists destroyed a hotel, killing guests. In the nearby Chabad House, a center for Orthodox Jews, terrorists killed a young Orthodox rabbi, Gavriel Holtzberg, and his wife, Rivka.

Toulouse, France: On March 19, 2012, a rabbi and three small children were murdered by an Algerian-French terrorist outside a Jewish school.

According to Suzan Johnson Cook, the US State Department's Ambassador for International Religious Freedom, the latest report of that organization exposed several violations, including the rise of anti-Semitism in nations from Venezuela to the Netherlands and an openly anti-Semitic political party in Hungary. [3]

No, anti-Semitism did not disappear following World War II. In fact, it seems to have grown exponentially and to have spread across the globe. It is no longer just a "European problem."

But why? Why have the Jewish people, above all others, suffered such rejection, hatred, and violence? Why have so many unprovoked attacks been leveled against innocent Jews?

1. The International Herald Tribune: Study shows persistence of anti-Semitic attitudes, January 25, 2012.

2. Aftenposten: Hatred of Jews in Oslo Schools June 12, 2011.

3. CBN News Report: "Rising anti-Semitism in Europe". Cbn.com. 7/31/12

CHAPTER 3

Anti-Semitism: A Spiritual Force

Anti-Semitism is a demonic force that has raised its ugly head throughout recorded history. This pervasive evil spirit did not manifest its thirst for innocent Jewish blood solely during the Spanish and Portuguese inquisitions or the pogroms of Russia, Poland, and other European countries. Nor did the genocide of 1942-45 bring an end to the persecution of Jews.

The manifestations of this power from hell can be found in the decrees of Pharaoh in Egypt, who ordered the babies of the Hebrews to be slaughtered, forcing Moses' mother to hide him in the bull-rushes. It was the insidious power behind Haman as he manipulated the Persian king, Ahasuerus to decree the death of all the Jews in his kingdom. Fortunately, Haman was brought down by Queen Esther, who risked her life to approach the king and thereby saved her people. This force was again the provocateur behind the enemies of Israel bringing about the wars so valiantly fought and won by King David. Herod's decree that all male babies in Bethlehem be put to death was another example of the working of the spirit of anti-Semitism.

Anti-Semitism, as with other demonic forces, is a false accuser. Lies propagated against the Jewish people have spread like a cancer over the centuries. These insinuations may take many forms:

Hitler justified persecution of Jews based on the rhetoric of "The Protocols of the Elders of Zion", a fabrication accusing Jews of conspiracy to control markets and governments worldwide.

In some countries, the Bible has been used to justify killing Jews. They were labeled "Christ killers," leading to pogroms in many countries of "Christian Europe" over the centuries.

In the Muslim world, the jihadist declaration "Death to the Zionist infidels" is a call to destroy the Jewish people and the Jewish nation of Israel.

Anti-Semitic attitudes pervade society behind the veil of propaganda, with claims such as: "I don't hate Jews. I just hate the nation of Israel."

One of the most deceptive forms of anti-Semitism is found in the church under the guise of "replacement theology." Through the manipulation of Scriptures, replacement theology implies that the Gentile church has taken the place of the Jews. Therefore God's promises are no longer applicable to the Jewish people but are now extended exclusively to the church.

Some of these attitudes are blatantly clear examples of hatred against the Jewish people. Others are masked in self-righteousness. But they all have the same root: the spirit of anti-Semitism.

As Paul wrote: "We wrestle not against flesh and blood, but against principalities, powers, spiritual wickedness in high places and the rulers of the present darkness" (Eph. 6:12 KJV.[1]

In every form of spiritual warfare, it is important for us to realize that we are not fighting against human beings, but against the strongholds of the enemy of our souls who seeks to control the minds of people. These demonic strongholds work in people's minds to cause them to believe lies. In the area of anti-Semitism, the lies are in the form of false accusations against Jewish people. Negative stereotypes and generalizations are used to create an ever-growing hatred of their victims.

But as intercessors and advocates, we are called to love our enemies, even the enemies of these Jewish victims. At the same time we must stand against the sin of anti-Semitism, being sure that it is thoroughly rooted out of our own lives. It is only by the power of the Holy Spirit and under the leading of the Lord that we can do so. Paul clearly describes the nature of our warfare:

> For though we live in the world, we do not wage war as the world does. The weapons we fight with are not the weapons of the world. On the contrary, they have divine power to demolish strongholds. We demolish arguments and every pretension that sets itself up against the knowledge of God and we take captive every thought to make it obedient to Christ.
> —2 Cor. 10:3–5 NIV[2]

In our stand against anti-Semitism, the first prerequisite is to understand that our battle is a spiritual one against demonic forces that have taken control of the minds of those willing to believe lies and stereotypes about the Jewish people. We must face the fight with faith, knowing that "greater is He that is in you than he that is in the world" 1 John 4:4KJV.[3] Since we are battling the very powers of hell in the struggle against anti-Semitic lies and accusations, we must look to a power greater than ourselves for the wisdom to "demolish arguments and every pretension that sets itself up" to create hatred against the Jews. God will give us the weapons we need for this battle, whether it be direction in prayer, books we should write, public stances that we need to take—whatever the need, the Lord will provide and guide us.

In recent years an unprecedented wave of hatred against Europe's few remaining Jews has been increasing exponentially. At times current sentiment toward the Jews has seemed reminiscent of Pre-Krystal Nacht Germany, 1938, shortly before the Holocaust began. This resurgence of anti-Semitism is being fostered both in society and through the media. It is imperative that the lessons of history be remembered. God forbid that believers remain silent as the majority of the church did during World War II. As the church currently represents the group most closely aligned with Israel and the Jewish people, it is incumbent upon believers to be informed about current trends and conditions regarding anti-Semitism. Knowledge is the fuel in the fight to counteract bigotry.

1. The Holy Bible: King James Version
2. The Holy Bible: New International Version
3. The Holy Bible: King James Version

CHAPTER 4

The Jews: God's Chosen, but for What?

God calls the Jewish people "the apple of His eye," (Zech. 2:8), "His own inheritance" (Deut. 9:29), and "the people He claims as His own" (Jer. 10:16).

When Abraham left his homeland in what is modern Iraq and journeyed to Canaan, today's Israel, God said He would give him and his descendants the land of Canaan as an everlasting inheritance (Gen. 12:7). Sara had not yet given birth to an heir. But Sara, at ninety, and Abraham, at one hundred, saw the promise of God fulfilled in the birth of Isaac. Isaac passed the inheritance of the land of Canaan to his son Jacob (Gen. 26:24) and not to Esau, his eldest son. Jacob fled his home after having tricked his father into giving him the blessing he intended for Esau. On his return journey to Canaan with his wives, children and livestock, Jacob had a meeting with God. During this visitation in Bethel, God changed Jacob's name to Israel. (Gen. 32:30–31) Under orders from the Lord, Jacob later returned to Bethel, the place of his first encounter with God. The Lord reaffirmed that his name was changed from Jacob to Israel.

> "Your name is Jacob. You shall no longer be called Jacob, but Israel shall be your name. Then he called him Israel. God also said to him, I am God Almighty. Be fruitful and multiply. A nation and a company of nations shall come from you.

And kings shall come forth from you. The land that I gave
Abraham and Isaac, I will give it to you. And I will give the
land to your descendents after you. Gen. 35: 10-12 NAS [1]

Satan knows the position of the nation of Israel and the Jews as
the chosen people of the Most High God. He is insanely jealous of the
Jewish people for this reason. Isaiah 14:12 says that Satan would exalt
himself above the Most High. He would have all worship and attention
for himself. In fact, Satan seeks to eliminate the Jewish people as God's
prophetic timepiece.

Satan knows that his end is at hand with the Jewish people's restoration
to the land of Israel. He knows that all the promises of the end time are
wrapped up in the nation of Israel and the Jewish people. Therefore, he
has focused the wrath of hell on the Jews and Israel over the centuries
in the form of persecution, much of which was perpetrated in the name
of Christ by the Church. In fact, Jewish people have difficulty hearing
about Jesus and Christianity due to all the suffering they have endured
at the hands of those who called themselves Christians.

Two thousand years ago, Jesus' disciples asked Him if He would
at that time restore the nation of Israel (Acts 1:6). They knew that,
according to the prophets, the restoration of Israel would be the sign of
the Messiah's coming. Moses, Jeremiah, Ezekiel, Daniel, and Zechariah
all had prophesied the restoration of the Jewish people to their homeland
from all nations. When the disciples asked Jesus this question, the land
was under the control of Rome. There hadn't been a Jewish kingdom
since the time of the Babylonian captivity. But in 1948, the promise
foreseen by the prophets came to pass. Israel is again a nation, and the
Jews have been regathered from all nations to their land.

Jews have come to Israel from Kaifang, China.

Jews immigrated in recent years from northern India where they
practiced circumcision with stones, according to biblical
practice. These Jews call themselves *Ben Manashe* and claim to
be the lost tribe of Manasseh.

Jews have come from the Americas, where they were driven as a
result of the Spanish Inquisition. (Many of the first European

inhabitants to the Americas were Jews fleeing Spanish and Portuguese persecution.)

Satan's jealousy has been manifested through world leaders speaking against the nation of Israel. In recent years, U.S. President Barack Obama has blatantly sided with the opponents of Israel. One advertisement in the Jerusalem Post showed a picture of Obama wearing a turban made from the Palestinian scarf, the *kefeya*. The caption read: "Mr. President, why do you want to kill us?"

Satanic hatred toward Israel has been demonstrated through propagandistic news media that slant reports on conflicts between Israel and her neighbors.

Iran

Currently, the most alarming threat against Israel is Iranian nuclear proliferation. The Ayatollah Ali Khameini, Iran's spiritual head, and Mahmoud Ahmadinejad, the president, have sworn that they (like their previous Persian counterpart, Haman) intend to destroy Israel. The God of Israel will defend His people, and woe unto those who would plot her destruction. Israel is faced with the urgency of bombing the nuclear plants in Isfahan, Fordo facility in Qom, and Natanz. But the United States and the rest of the Mideast quartet—the United Nations, Russia, and the European Union—oppose bombing and want to use sanctions. Sanctions are only buying Iran more time to fortify nuclear installations in underground bunkers that cannot be reached by conventional weaponry.

Iran's leadership embraces a teaching that concerns the Mahdi, or twelfth Imam. The Mahdi supposedly has lived at the bottom of a well outside Tehran for many centuries. This messianic figure is supposed to return and make the whole world Muslim after a cataclysmic destruction of much of the earth. Ahmadinejad has declared that he is the chosen vessel to bring about this destruction through nuclear weapons and to usher in the Mahdi. He has declared that his first target for destruction will be the Zionist entity, Israel.

Many would view Ahmadinejad's threats against Israel and the Jews as simply the ravings of a madman. Most Western leaders treated Hitler's threats in the 1930s in the same way.

The Muslim Brotherhood and the caliphate

The Muslim Brotherhood is making every effort to establish a caliphate, or Muslim empire, across the Middle East and North Africa. What Western governments and news media naively call the "Arab Spring" movement for freedom may actually be a diabolical plan by the Muslim Brotherhood to gain control over a large landmass in the Middle East. This would enable the group to reestablish the lost caliphate. A caliphate is a conglomeration of nations joined under the umbrella of a theocratic Islamic government, practicing shariah law.

The unrest and upheaval throughout the Arab and Muslim world should not be deemed a "democratic movement," as many have called it. There is an insidious power behind it with a frightening agenda that has come right out of the strategizing rooms of hell. The so-called democratic Arab Spring has been instigated by the Muslim Brotherhood, which has openly declared its goal of world domination.

Hamas: An enemy from within

It isn't necessary to search extensively for the true goals of the Muslim Brotherhood and the Islamic revolution. A review of the Hamas charter sheds light on the subject. The terrorist group is the offspring of the Muslim Brotherhood. The Hamas covenant, written in 1988, illuminates the true intentions of the group toward Israel and the non-Muslim world.

> Article 7 states that the movement is a worldwide one. This would indicate that the tentacles of Hamas are indeed international. A global strategy is apparent and is operative through the Muslim Brotherhood.

Article 11's second and third paragraphs state that Hamas will never give "Palestine" (Israel) to the Jews. It is fair to assume that there will never be a peace treaty to which Hamas agrees, no matter how much land Israel concedes.

Article 13 states that Hamas will accept no peace conference to negotiate a treaty and declares that peace negotiations are a waste of time. Yet the trend in the Mideast quartet is to legitimize Hamas as a relevant partner in the so-called peace talks despite the fact that Hamas has been a major source of terrorist operations in the decades since its inception.

Article 14 declares that it is the duty of all Muslims to liberate Palestine. It is apparent that this is a call to world jihad on behalf of the Palestinians.

Article 22 declares the rest of the world the enemy of Hamas and condemns the non-Muslim world for being behind World War I, which brought about the destruction of the caliphate. In this paragraph, Hamas issues a challenge to capitalism and communism as well.

Article 30 is a call for writers, educators, media people, intelligentsia of all backgrounds and all those in positions of authority to use their influence on behalf of the Islamic resistance movement. Thus, a formidable propaganda machine has been set in place that has effectively influenced world opinion against Israel. (See Chapter 13.)

Article 31 states that Muslims, Jews, and Christians can exist peacefully together, but they must all be under the control of Islam and sharia law. Hamas, like the Qur'an, espouses the subjugation and destruction of the non-Muslim world.

Article 32 refers to Zionist expansionism and claims that the Jews want to take over the entire Middle East. This accusation seems to come right out of *The Protocols of the Elders of Zion,* a book that fanned the flames of anti–Semitism in the early nineteen hundreds and helped prepare the way for the Holocaust. This hoax, supposedly the work of world Jewish leaders, was written in Russia in 1903 and disseminated throughout Europe in a number of translations. Five-hundred thousand copies were then distributed in English throughout the United States, financed by Henry Ford. Although the book was proven to be a fabrication, Hitler made it part of the curriculum in German schools after 1933. This book was Hitler's major justification for the genocide of the Jewish people. [2]

World caliphate conferences

Hizb ut-Tahrir is an international Islamic organization whose goal is the establishment of a worldwide caliphate ruled by shariah law. To this end, the group sponsors conferences in major world capitals. In March of 2012, a conference was held in Vienna with the theme "Caliphate: The State Model of the Future." Similar conferences were held in Belgium in March of 2012, the Netherlands in 2011, and Chicago in 2010. Hizb ut-Tahrir was created in 1953 by a Palestinian judge and calls for the dismantling of Israel, which it considers an illegal entity. The group is active in the United Kingdom, Arab and Central Asian countries, Indonesia, and the United States. (See www.hizbuttahrir.org.) [3]

The implications of a caliphate under shariah law were presented in an interview conducted by Christian leader, Rick Joyner who questioned Kamal Saleem, a former radical Muslim who is now a Christian. Saleem revealed that under shariah law women are not allowed to inherit property. All inherited property from a woman's parents goes to her husband, according to the Qur'an. Saleem said the Qur'an states that the fire of hell is fueled by women. Under shariah, women must have four witnesses to prove a matter in court, while men need only two. Recently, a fourteen-year-old girl who had been raped by her uncle in Pakistan could not produce witnesses. In the shariah court, the girl was found guilty of adultery and executed while her uncle was acquitted. Saleem said that hundreds of thousands of women have been murdered in "honor killings," which are legal under shariah. These women may have dated a Westerner or may have been suspected of illicit sex. The families are immediately acquitted merely by claiming that the murder of a woman was an "honor killing."

Saleem reported that schools in Saudi Arabia teach children how to cut off the hands and feet of a thief and how to subjugate women. Once when Saleem was in Saudi Arabia, he was herded into a square with a group of people after Friday prayers to watch as authorities cut off prisoners' hands, cut out their tongues, and gouged out the eyes of the convicted. On the same occasion, he saw six men beheaded after being accused of homosexuality.

Hizb ut-Tahrir and the caliphate

Hizb ut Tahrir's web site advocates a violent struggle against Israel over Gaza: "Lifting the siege of Gaza will never happen through condemnation or Hajj to the UN. It can only ever happen through mobilization of the armies that surround the 'Jewish entity' as a bracelet encircles a wrist." (The term "Jewish entity" refers to the state of Israel.)

Hizb ut Tahrir calls for military action to conquer Al-Quds (Arabic for Jerusalem):

"Al Quds cannot be liberated by demonstration or sit in ... it can only be restored by mobilizing armed forces to eliminate the Jewish entity!'"

During a meeting last year of the Conservative Political Action Conference, John Bolton, the former US ambassador to the United Nations, told a reporter: "There are leaders in that part of the world who do, like Osama bin Laden, talk about the restoration of the caliphate ... I am very disturbed by that because that kind of radical ideology ... threatens moderate Muslim and Arab regimes that are important to American national security interests."

The Muslim Brotherhood

Hizb ut-Tahrir and Hamas are not the only groups advocating the establishment of a global Muslim state or caliphate. The leader of the Muslim Brotherhood expressed the same desire in 1995. On February 9, 2011, *The Jerusalem Post* reported on translations of a book published in 1995 by the fifth leader of the Muslim Brotherhood, Mustafa Mashhur, in which the ultimate goal of the organization was revealed: a global caliphate (Mustafa Mashhur, *The Laws of Da'wa,* 1995). [4]

President Obama and Secretary of State Hillary Clinton have declared that the Muslim Brotherhood is a viable negotiation partner in the reorganization of Egypt's government after the Brotherhood worked with leaders of the "Arab Spring" revolution to oust Hosni Mubarak. The Brotherhood had promised not to influence the election, but put up one of its own as a candidate for president who has now won office as the leader of Egypt.

In an article titled "The Arab Spring to Caliphate: Echoes of a Medieval Polemic," appearing in *Eurasia Review* on March 5, 2012,[5] proposes that the Muslim Brotherhood has played on the image of the fall of communism after glasnost. However, an oppressive fate awaits those countries that have overthrown their dictators (meaning Libya, Egypt, Tunisia, and Yemen). That fate is assimilation into a conglomerate state under radical shariah law. Western entities that have backed the so-called liberation movement and endorsed the Muslim Brotherhood as a peaceful force for creating a Western-style democracy are terribly deceived. The ultimate goal of this movement is a world caliphate with all nations under shariah law. Those who do not comply, according to the Qur'an, should be executed.

Al Jazeera is the Muslim news station and propaganda machine for the Muslim Brotherhood, according to television commentator Glenn Beck. Listeners of the station who follow Al Jazeera in both English and Arabic explain that what is broadcast on the station in English is selected to appease Westerners, while what is said in Arabic reveals radical Islamic rhetoric. The English broadcasts tend to downplay the real goals of the Muslim Brotherhood and other radical groups, while the Arabic broadcasts stoke the fires of hatred against Israel, the Jews, the United States, and Western-style democracy.

Hassan al-Banna, the founder of the Muslim Brotherhood, stated the strategic goals of the organization in gaining a global presence: "Begin with reform of the individual, then start building the family and society, then the government; then the rightly guided caliphate, then instructing the world; instructing guidance, wisdom, truth and justice" [6] It is clear from this clearly designed agenda that the group's strategy is to start small but aim for "global takeover".

God's chosen people: Survival in the midst of such enemies

Little Israel is a nation surrounded by 250 million enemies. Not only governments of Muslim nations but many global organizations are bent on Israel's destruction. Israel's allies, even the United States, waffle in their support of the tiny country in accordance with the demands of Arab oil magnates. While there is more than enough oil in Alaska to support America's needs for many generations, the current administration, under the guise of environmental conservation, will not allow development of this resource. Is this due to agreements with Arab partners? It is clear that the strategists of hell who seek the destruction of the Jewish state are relentlessly working to achieve their dastardly goals, and to do so they would seek to use global leaders. But what are the implications of these trends for those who are called to "Comfort ye my people" and "Speak ye comfortably to Jerusalem"?

1. 1. The Holy Bible: New American Standard Version.
2. **2.** *Hamas Covenant:* Yale University, Lillian Goldman Library, 1988.
3. **3.** See www.hizbuttahrir.org.)
4. **4.** Mustafa Mashhur, *The Laws of Da'wa,* Dar al Tawziah war-Nashr al Islamia (Islamic Publishing House) Al Sayeda Zalnob Square 8, Cairo, Egypt, 1995. Translation by: Palestinian Media Watch.
5. **5.** Lais, Hasmet: "The Arab Spring to Caliphate: Echoes of a Medieval Polemic," in *Eurasia Review,* Mar. 5, 2012
6. 6. *Jihad watch.org,* Feb. 2012.

CHAPTER 5

What Does This Have to Do with the Church?

The opposite of love isn't hate. The opposite of love is indifference.
Elie Wiesel, Nobel Peace Prize Recipient

As Gentile Christians, believers in Jesus, the Jewish Messiah, we have been made a part of the people of Israel. Romans 11:23 says we have been "grafted" into the tree of Israel. When one plant is grafted into another, the two become one new plant. Paul implies that our very identity is tied into the destiny and welfare of the Jewish people. It is through them that we have been given the prophets, the Bible, the law, and our Messiah, Jesus. All that we have, spiritually, has come through this people.

Believers in Jesus, the Jewish Messiah share a great heritage with the Jewish people. Having been made joint-heirs with Jesus, and heirs to the promises of Abraham through our Lord's atonement, we share an inheritance with the Jewish people. We have been made part of God's family – both Jew and Gentile. Consequently, Gentile believers are to care for the welfare of the Jewish people and the nation of Israel, as we would for our own family. We are called to aid Jews as they return to the land of Israel according to Isaiah 49. We are to bless them, to comfort them and to pray for the peace of their capital, Jerusalem. The instructions concerning Israel and our obligations relating to the Jewish people represent a mandate to all Gentile believers in Jesus.

Silence is complicity: German Christians and the Jews

With the exception of Dietrich Bonhoeffer, his colleagues, and a few Christians, the church of Germany and the majority of Germans remained silent during the persecution of the Jewish people during World War II. As the machinery of the Final Solution was set in place and Nazi gatherings, Reich media propaganda, and Krystal Nacht clearly revealed Hitler's plan for the Jews, the church of Germany sat in denial and silent complicity. Hitler had been blustering against the Jews for years and demonstrated his intentions on November 8-9, 1938, called "Krystal Nacht", or the night of broken glass, the start of the Holocaust. During the pogrom that began on that night, synagogues and Jewish shops were razed. Jewish homes were vandalized, Jews were arrested and deportation to concentration camps began. Following this fateful event, life became intolerably difficult for the Jews of Germany and Austria. They were no longer allowed to conduct business. Jewish children were forbidden to go to school or were forced into schools for Jews only. And more and more Jews were 'disappearing" throughout the Reich.

Meanwhile, under the leadership of Bishop Ludwig Müller, the German Evangelical Church was formed during this time. Müller sought to "Aryanize" the church by removing the Old Testament and many references to the Jewish traditions of the New Testament. The majority of the believers sat in indifference as this new German "sect" emerged. [1].

A minority of Christians rebelled against the state church. The "Confessing Church" was formed. They continued Biblically based Bible instruction and many worked to save the lives of Jews. But what happened to the rest of the Church?

On January 20, 1942, the Wannsee Conference took place. It was in this secret meeting in a town near Berlin that fifteen Nazi leaders decided the fate of European Jewry. The result was that more than six million innocent Jews, two-thirds of the world's Jewish population, were slaughtered. All of this happened while Christians in Germany, Austria and other European countries went on with their lives as if nothing were out of the ordinary.

Such denial is commonplace in genocide. Consider the catastrophe of abortion in the United States, Europe, and many other parts of the world. Millions of babies are being murdered throughout the world, and very few people are doing anything about it. Life goes on as usual.

Denial was the rule for the Christians of Germany and Austria during the Holocaust. Similarly, the Christians of medieval Europe found it "acceptable" to hate Jews and kill them as punishment for being "Christ killers" or under the false accusation of blood-libel crimes. I have talked to Jewish people in Europe who can't bear to hear a church organ because of the fact that for many centuries organ music was used to drown out the screams of Jews being tortured in churches. Not only has the church been silent and indifferent, we have been complicit.

We need to pray that our eyes will be opened to our complicity in the injustices being committed against the Jewish people and the nation of Israel. One of my dear Jewish friends recently told me: "We Jews have begun to realize that the best friends we have today are the Christians." Although it is a tragedy to imagine that the Jewish people meet with so much opposition, it is wonderful to see that change is taking place in the relationship between Christians and Jews. Every Christian must rise up on behalf of Jesus' brethren and stand with them and with the nation of Israel in their fight for existence.

A proper course of action

On October 1, 1943, during the German occupation of Denmark, Hitler issued orders for Denmark's Jews to be arrested and deported to death camps. The bishops of the church of Denmark took an extraordinary stand. As the heads of the Danish state church, they authorized Bishop Hans Fuglsang-Damgaard to write a letter that would be sent throughout the country. The letter spelled out why the people of Denmark, as a Christian nation, should stand against the persecution of the Jews. "A Letter expressing the Church of Denmark's position concerning the Jews" was read on October 3, 1943, in all of Danmark's churches: [2]

Everywhere, where persecutions of Jews are taking place due to racial or religious reasons, it is the duty of the Christian church to protest against it.

1. Because we should never be able to forget that the Lord of the church, Jesus Christ, was born in Bethlehem of the Virgin Mary in accordance with God's promise to his own people, Israel. The history of the Jewish people until the birth of Christ consists of the preparation to that salvation, which God has given for all people through Christ. This is signified by the Old Testament, which is a part of our Bible.

2. Because the persecution of Jews contradicts the Church of Jesus Christ's message of human compassion and charity. Christ is no respecter of persons, and he has taught us to see that every human life is precious in the eyes of God.

3. Because it contradicts the concept of justice, which is possessed by the Danish people, enshrined in our Danish–Christian culture throughout the centuries. In accordance with this, all Danish citizens have, through the words of the constitution, an equal right and responsibility before the law and are guaranteed freedom of religion. We perceive freedom of religion as being the right to practice our worship after being called to service and conscience, so that race and religion may never alone serve as an occasion to depriving a man of the right to liberty and property. Regardless of difference in religious views, we will fight to ensure that our Jewish brothers and sisters retain the same liberty which we ourselves value higher than life itself.

There exists among the Danish church's leaders a clear understanding of our duty to be law-abiding citizens, which does not mean that we will not respect those who have authority over us, but at the same time we are, by our conscience, compelled to enforce the law and protest against any violation of law (concerning human rights). Therefore, we will in this context unequivocally acknowledge that we must obey God over man when these laws are violated. **2**.

As a result of the bishops' action, 99 percent of Denmark's Jews survived the Holocaust. Under the inspiration of Bishop Fuglsang-Damgaard's letter, the people of Denmark worked through the night. They used fishing boats and every sort of sea craft to carry the Jews of Denmark out of the country to safety in Sweden.

A precedent for our time:

Each of us must ask this question: What would I have done if I had been living in Europe at that time? The answer to this question lies in your response to another question: What am I doing today to stem the tide of anti-Semitism? Unfortunately, there is very little difference in people's attitudes between Hitler's time and today.

Across Europe, a remnant took a stand against the hideous injustice and evil being committed against the Jewish people. These courageous few risked their lives and the lives of their families to respond righteously by saving Jewish lives. Who were they, and how did they make the decision to choose the action they took?

1. Barnett, Victoria. For the Soul of the People: Protestant Protest against Hitler. Oxford University Press, 1992, pg. 33.

2. Fuglsang–Damgaard, Hans: "A Letter expressing the Church of Denmark's position concerning the Jews, Archives: Danish Museum of the Holocaust. Oct., 1943. Translation: Martha Smith.

CHAPTER 6

The Resistance: The Righteous of the Nations

Those who resisted Hitler to save Jewish lives were in the minority. But they are worthy of honor for their valor. The resistance, whether from the perspective of faith or sheer moral conviction, was a formidable force against fascism. The majority of good, church-going people were silent. They lived in denial and self-deception and were not willing to face the reality of Hitler's intentions. Perhaps this was out of fear of punishment if they would be caught. Or perhaps it was due to latent anti-Semitic attitudes which were pervasive in the culture. After all, anti-Semitism was a "politically correct" point of view.

But to be silent when faced with anti-Semitism and attacks on the Jewish people is not only to be compliant but to be participant. The Bible says that to know to do right and not to do it is sin. We have only two choices: we can be part of the problem or part of the solution. We can resist and stand against anti-Semitism while standing for righteousness, no matter what the cost. Or we can be silent and therefore become part of the evil.

This choice lies before each of us as attacks on Jews and the nation of Israel increase worldwide. Those who chose to fight against Nazism and for the survival of the Jewish people in World War II may serve as role models for us as we approach a decision to do rightly.

VOICES OF THE RESISTANCE [1]

Magde Trocme's story

"As descendants of the Huguenots, our people were familiar with persecution and understood the need to flee from oppression. As the Jews came flooding into our district of France seeking refuge, we were ready. My husband Andre was the pastor of the congregation in the Evangelical Temple of Le Chambon sur Lignon. Sunday after Sunday, Andre urged our congregants to help 'the people of the book.' 'Receive them in your homes, feed them, protect them. They are the apple of God's eye. Has He not said, "I will bless them that bless you and curse them that curse you"?'

"Andre and I worked side by side. My duties were to locate families in the surrounding villages who would hide the Jewish people in their homes or barns. They came from Germany, Belgium, Poland, and from within our own country. Farmers, townspeople, boarding schools, orphanages— every means possible was employed to save the Jews from deportation and death. All told, around five thousand Jews were rescued here in our area as a result of Andre's influence.

"One day in February 1943, my husband and two of his colleagues were arrested by the Gestapo and imprisoned near Limoges. Andre was held for interrogation for five weeks. After his release, he had to go underground for the rest of the war.

"Our nephew, Daniel Trocme, a teacher of physics and science at La Roche, a prestigious boarding school in Verneuil, became immersed in activity for the resistance in 1941. At that time my husband Andre asked Daniel to leave his position and to take over Les Grillons, a boarding school for Jewish children. Daniel cared for the children as if they were his own. He would read to them at night when they went to bed. At night he could be found long after bedtime repairing children's shoes with a hammer and nails.

"Some months later, Daniel returned to La Roche to work as the principal and continued hiding Jewish children. In June of 1943 the Gestapo raided La Roche to search for Daniel and the Jewish students. Our nephew was not at home, but when he returned and found that the Jewish students were taken, Daniel turned himself in to the Gestapo to be with the children. In April of 1944, Daniel, aged 34, died in the gas chambers of Majdanek concentration camp.

"What was it that drove us to risk our lives? Jesus said, Inasmuch as you have done it unto these my brethren (the Jewish people), you have done it unto me. How could we not give everything to save them when we love Him more than anything else in the world?"

> There is no price too great
> We could pay to counter hate.
> To save the oppressed from their hand,
> To bring down tyranny and fight for liberty,
> The redemption of our land.
>
> With the help of Almighty God,
> We will conquer this enemy,
> We will see deliverance come,
> To those in captivity,
> We are willing to offer all,
> To heed His holy call,
> To see the evil fall
> And set the captives free.
> —Magda's song, *Voices of the Resistance*

Photo by permission of Yad Vashem
Jean Moulin, French Resistance Leader

Jean Moulin's story

"I am hunted at the same time by Vichy and the Gestapo who are not unaware of my identity, nor my activities. My task is becoming more and more delicate, while the difficulties increase constantly. I am determined to hold on as long as possible, but if I should disappear, I should not have had the time to familiarize my successors with the necessary information." These words were penned by Jean Moulin, leader of the French Resistance, in 1943, shortly before his death.

He knew it wouldn't be long. He saw the shadowy figures of the Gestapo hiding to watch his every move. Yet, as a sworn pacifist, Moulin would not carry a gun or seek to defend himself by killing others.

He was no stranger to the cruelties of the Gestapo. The Germans had arrested him in June of 1940 when he would not sign a document that accused Senegalese French troops of committing civilian massacres. While in prison, he attempted suicide by cutting his throat with a piece of glass. For the rest of his life, he wore a scarf to hide the scar. That is how he is remembered.

In November of 1941, under the name of Joseph Jean Mercier, Moulin met with Gen. Charles de Gaulle in London. He was asked to return to France to unify the independent resistance groups operating throughout France. Moulin returned to France on January 1, 1942, by a parachute drop over the Alps. His code names were Rex and Max as he met with the leaders from resistance organizations: Combat, Liberation, Franc-Tireur, Front National, Comité d'Action Socialiste. His leadership provided the impetus needed to turn the French Resistance into the most powerful force in Europe against the Nazi regime.

But Moulin's days were numbered, and in June of 1943 he was captured at a meeting of the resistance in Caluire-et-Cuire in Rhone. He was interrogated in Lyons by Klaus Barbie, head of the Gestapo there, and later in Paris. He never revealed anything to his captors. He died on a train near Metz as he was being transported to a concentration camp. His death was most likely from a beating at Barbie's hands or from suicide.

Jean Moulin brought unity among the resistance groups and saved France from the civil wars that ravaged Poland, Yugoslavia, and Greece. He gave his battered nation back its dignity. Though Moulin never carried a gun or blew up a train, he single-handedly unified the French Resistance into a veritable army.

Photo by permission of Yad Vashem
Irene Sendlerowa

Irene Sendlerowa's story

"How can we save the children? Something must be done." This must have been the question in the heart of Irena Sendlerowa and her colleagues in the Polish underground group Zegota. Living in Warsaw, Sendlerowa watched as the brick walls were being built to enclose the ghetto, imprisoning many thousands of Jewish people under orders of the Third Reich. She and her colleagues knew that the innocents behind those walls were awaiting certain death.

Sendlerowa began working to help Jewish people in Warsaw shortly after the invasion of Poland by the Germans in 1939. She and her colleagues made three thousand false passports for Jewish families. In doing so, they were risking their own lives.

When Zegota was formed, Sendlerowa, under the code name of Jolanta, became the head of the children's division. Only those with special permission could go in and out of the Warsaw ghetto. As a social worker, Sendlerowa gained access by checking for typhus in the ghetto. When she got past the checkpoint and was well within the walls, Sendlerowa would put on an arm band carrying the Jewish star to show her solidarity. She then convinced Jewish mothers to let her take their babies and small children out of the ghetto and place them with Polish Catholic families or in convents and orphanages to save their lives. She carried the babies out in coffins, luggage, packages, trolleys, ambulances, or any other means possible. She wrote the names of the children and their parents on slips of paper that she placed in a glass jar and buried under an apple tree in her backyard.

Sendlerowa and twenty-four other workers from the Zegota movement, smuggled two thousand-five hundred babies out of the Warsaw ghetto to safe refuge before the inhabitants were placed on trains and taken to death camps to be annihilated.

Sendlerowa and her co-workers in the children's division of the resistance were eventually arrested and sentenced to death. She was the only one from her segment of Zegota to survive. The others were executed. After being cruelly beaten, Sendlerowa was left in the forest to die. She was found by resistance workers who had bribed her would-be executioners to release her. Irene had been tortured and was left unconscious. Her legs and arms were broken. Irena was then taken by Zegota workers to a hiding place where she spent the rest of the war. Working from her place of seclusion until liberation, she continued to direct efforts to rescue Jewish children and families.

After the war, Sendlerowa dug up the jar with the names of the family members of the rescued children. Unfortunately, it was impossible to reconnect many of the children with their families, since most had been killed in Treblinka or other death camps.

Irena Sendlerowa was nominated for the Nobel Peace Prize in 2007, losing to Al Gore and his film on global warming. Sendlerowa has been honored among the "Righteous of the Nations" in Yad Vashem in Jerusalem.

In 2008, Sendlerowa died at ninety-seven. Her Christian faith was the power behind her acts of heroism and sacrifice. Such deeds would be possible only through divine strength. Sendlerowa had a heart filled with love and compassion, and she was willing to offer her very life to do what she knew to be right. When she was honored by the Polish parliament for her wartime efforts, she said, "Every child saved with my help is the justification of my existence on earth, not a title to glory."

Photo by permission of Yad Vashem
Dietrich Bonhoeffer

Dietrich Bonhoeffer's story

"Only the obedient believe. If we are to believe, we must obey God, even if it means death." This was the teaching of the theologian and German resistance leader Dietrich Bonhoeffer.

At twenty-one, Bonhoeffer was awarded a doctorate in theology from the University of Berlin. He studied for one year in New York City at Union Theological Seminary and then traveled to India to study nonviolent resistance under Mahatma Gandhi.

Returning to Germany shortly before the war, Bonhoeffer withdrew his membership from the Lutheran Church because most of the churches in Germany were either complicit with Hitler or were silent out of fear of reprisals. He became a pastor and a leader in the Confessing Church and insisted that the organization strongly oppose Hitler's policies toward the Jewish people. Eventually the Nazis forbade Bonhoeffer to speak publicly or to preach.

He began to work with a group of military leaders in resistance operations. The group was active in smuggling Jews out of the country and in gathering military intelligence for Allied forces. In April of 1943, Bonhoeffer was arrested for having transferred funds to Switzerland that would be used to help relocate Jewish refugees. As a result, he spent a year and a half in prison.

When he was free again, Bonhoeffer worked with several high-ranking German military officers developing plans for the assassination of Hitler and for the eventual liberation of Germany. When the assassination attempt failed, Bonhoeffer and the others involved were arrested. They were sent to concentration camps, tortured, and finally executed. Dietrich Bonhoeffer was hanged, together with several generals, an admiral, and other resistance leaders, on April 9, 1945, one month before Germany's surrender.

When most of the Christians of his homeland were silent or supported Hitler, Bonhoeffer showed the world the reality of true obedience to God, even the call to offer one's life.

Photo courtesy Corrie Ten
Boom Association

Corrie Ten Boom

Corrie Ten Boom's story

"I have often pondered the story of the young widow Ruth, a Moabitess, who would leave her people to care for her aged mother-in-law, a Jew. In our family, it was as natural as breathing to love the Jewish people. You believe in the God of the Bible, you call yourself Christian, you love his chosen people—as simple as that. But not many in Holland at that time agreed with us.

"I remember once when a pastor came to visit my father shortly before we were arrested.

'You shouldn't be hiding Jews in your home,' the pastor said. 'You know the Bible says it is your duty to obey the authorities.'

"But my father wouldn't bow to him. 'I obey the authorities as long as they don't trespass the laws of God. But when they do, then I obey God,' Father responded.

"But you know it's dangerous for you to hide them. If they catch you, both you and your Jews will be sent to a concentration camp,' the pastor replied.

"I am prepared to help this people in any way I can, and if need be to die for them.' With these words, Father closed the discussion. How prophetic his words were.

"My brother, Willem, was the leader of the Dutch underground even before the invasion of Holland. After the Germans invaded, my sister Betsey, Father and I were mobilized. A secret hiding place was created behind the closet in my bedroom.

"When the Germans came to arrest us, they stormed through the little house, destroying everything in their path as they tried to find our Jewish guests. But the Jews remained hidden. Unknown to the Germans, our guests were ushered to safety some days later.

"Betsey, Father, and I were taken to Gestapo headquarters for interrogation. Father died there. A few days later, Betsey and I were transported by cattle car to Ravensbruck, a concentration camp. Betsey died of starvation and exhaustion in the camp. I was the only survivor among the three of us.

"At last I understood the anguish of Ruth in her widowhood as she gave herself to serve her Jewish mother-in-law. 'Where you go I will go. Where you lodge, I will lodge. Thy people will be my people and thy God will be my God. Where you die, there will I die, and also be buried.'

Ole Hallesby and Hans Christian Mamen

"I had often heard his name mentioned throughout my childhood. He was a renowned professor of theology and a well-respected author. When I went to study theology, I was excited to be able to take classes with Professor Ole Hallesby, a man whom all of Norway held in high regard.

"One day after class Hallesby came over to me and asked to speak to me privately. I was a bit surprised, and couldn't imagine why he would want to talk to me. Hallesby glanced around to make sure that the other students had left the room. He then looked into my eyes in silence, as if he were trying to read my thoughts. He said, 'I know that you have been volunteering on the frontier in Finland in the war against the Russians and you are a battle-wise young man. Hans Christian, would you be willing to escort Jewish refugees through the forests to safety in Sweden as a courier? If you are caught, it could cost you your life. You may be shot or sent to a concentration camp. What do you think?'

"I didn't hesitate for a minute. As a Christian, I felt that it was my duty to stand against evil and injustice. And besides that, I was just plain mad that the Nazis had invaded Norway and taken over our country. We all had to do everything we could to fight them.

"My first assignment was to escort two Jewish men and a Jewish woman through the forests and tundra to our contacts in Sweden. The first part of the trip was on a bus. Passports and IDs were checked on every form of public transport. Jewish passports had been stamped inside with a J for *Jewish*. When the inspector asked for our passports, the men put their thumbs over the J's inside. But the woman couldn't seem to find her passport. She fumbled through her purse for a long time. The man said he would come back. When he did, she didn't think to cover the J inside the document. The man saw the passport and said it was in order and went on. I knew that either he was in the resistance or God had blinded his eyes. Otherwise, we would have been arrested and sent to a concentration camp.

"I continued helping Jews to the border for two years until the Gestapo showed up at my mother's home to arrest me. She said that I wasn't home, and as soon as everything was clear she called the university and asked a colleague to convey a message to me: 'Pack your bag.' That was the signal we had agreed upon should the Gestapo come looking for me. My fiancée Ruth insisted on accompanying me across the border. When we arrived, we were met by a Nazi sympathizer. But miraculously, he let us go. Finally, we came to Stockholm where we spent the rest of the war years.

"However, Professor Hallesby, my esteemed mentor, didn't fare as well as we did. He was one of the major leaders in the rebellion of the church of Norway. The Quisling government insisted that the priests and the teachers throughout the country teach Nazi propaganda from the pulpits and in the schools. Hallesby organized a strike throughout the whole Norwegian church. The teachers joined the strike. Most of the Norwegian priests and teachers were then taken to concentration camps as a result of their civil disobedience. Ole Hallesby spent the next two years in Grini concentration camp outside of Oslo.

"When the war was over, Ole Hallesby continued his work as a professor of theology and a preacher. I returned to Norway with my wife Ruth to serve as a priest.

"Some people have said that we resistance workers were heroes. I have never thought of myself as a hero, and I am sure that Ole Hallesby didn't either. We just did the right thing. How could we have lived with ourselves if we hadn't taken the action we felt was right? How could anyone?"

LEA VILLAIN'S STORY

"My name is Jeanne, I'm 6 years old. I live with my family in Belgium. Mamma and Pappa say I talk too much, but I don't think so. I do like to talk, I must say. I'm so curious about everything and I like to know everything. Do you think I talk too much? There are so many things I don't understand. For example, why is it that Mamma and Pappa are always whispering so that I can't hear what they are saying? Why is it that all our visitors are named Mr. Smith or Mrs. Smith? Why don't they ever have another name? Why can't Iréne come outside the house and play with me? Why is it that I must share my bed with Iréne and her mother? Mamma and Pappa often go away from home for many days. So, Mary, the mother of Iréne, takes care of Iréne, my big sister, my brother, the baby and me. Mary is very nice but she always looks frightened and anxious.

"Another thing I don't understand is why Mamma and Pappa are so often angry with me. My older sister never gets a spanking, nor does my little brother. And my parents never scold my brother Fernand– well, at least not as much as me. It's always me who is in trouble.

"But when I'm with the boys in the street, I'm the boss! I love being with the boys. We climb trees, play soldiers and fight. I always win! Iréne is a girl with frills and ruffles. I like Iréne, but I would not like to be dressed with all that delicate lace stuff. I like to dress in pants like the boys. But I do miss my beautiful black patent leather shoes. They were so pretty! They had a small bow on the side. But my mother took them. She said they were too small. I think they fit me very well. These shoes I have now are awful. They didn't even tie. I wonder where mamma hid my shoes. They must be somewhere! Here? or there? No. Maybe they're in the trash. But where can they be? Oh ... Perhaps they're on top of the armoire? Of course, mom thinks I'm too small to get up there, but I'm used to climbing! I'm sure she's put them on top of the armoire!

"Ah! Voila! Ooooh! Look at these pretty little shiny balls? I wonder what they are? And what are these papers? And that? Gosh! A gun! Like playing war with the boys! But ours are made of wood. It would be more fun to play this. I will show this stuff to our neighbor, Lucienne. I'm sure she'd like to look at what I have found on the top of the armoire.

"Eh! Lucienne? Are you home? She's gone ... Oh ... something smells good! That's right, it's Friday, the day for mussels ... I'm sure Lucienne wouldn't mind if I ate a few."

"When she was a little girl, my friend Jeanne was always talking, always asking questions, and always in trouble! She didn't know that the husband of Lucienne was a collaborator. Lucienne, herself, was a patriot, and fortunately, on that day when Jeanne came by to show her the booty from on top of the armoire, Lucienne's husband was not home. After collecting the shiny bullets, the revolver, and the clandestine resistance leaflets from Jeanne, Lucienne was quick to return them to Lea, Jeanne's mother, the grandmother of my dear friend, Ardoine. When Fernand, Jeanne's father, came home and heard what Jeanne had done, he gave her a spanking, took her hand, opened it, put a bullet in it, and told her: "if you continue to speak, you know what will happen? The Germans will get your pappa, your mamma and your brothers and your sister and they will kill us all. They will take Irène and her family to a concentration camp where they will die. As for you, they will always give you lots of chocolate and candy, so you will speak again and again. Then they can kill more people because of you. Is that what you want? Do you want to be left alone without your family? If you do not hold your tongue, this is what your pappa will do. He will put the bullet in your hand, and it will explode!

After that, Jeanne remained silent for the first time in her life. But her parents had to quickly move the family into another house. This would have been necessary anyway, as Lea, who was actively typing newspapers for the resistance could be easily heard through the night hours. Lucienne and other neighbors warned the family that their activities had become common knowledge and may have been reported to the Gestapo.

After the move, Lea and Fernand were able to continue their work as officers of the Belgian Army, then the shadow army. Fernand had a secret room in the house to allow the Jewish family they sheltered and other Jews they were protecting to hide in an emergency. (Although they were given other names, Jeanne later learned that the family was named Smolovitch.)

Fernand and Lea regularly went on missions at night to make plans for resistance operations in Belgium and France and to pass information to other resistance groups. But gradually, the noose was tightening around them. In 1943, they no longer said, "If you get caught, but when you will be taken ...". After returning from a mission in France, Fernand and Lea realized they had been betrayed. To return to Belgium, they had to cross the border at a chapel, bordered by a stream. It was winter, the night was dark and it was stormy. Suddenly Fernand heard the voices of Germans looking for them. They had no other recourse but to lie down in the icy water of a creek in silence, as they did not know for sure if they were on the right side of the border. Suddenly, lightning flashed, illuminating the chapel. Then they saw men who were waiting, saying, "We were told they had to go through here. A man and a woman are trying to esape! The information was clear! "... Fernand and Lea then knew that they had been betrayed, but thanks to the flash of the lightning, they saw that they were on the right side of the border and managed to escape without making any noise. Lea had, however, caught a cold in the icy water. Because of the lack of food and the deprivation she had suffered, she could not recover. She developed tuberculosis and heart disease which brought about her death at age 48, a few years after the war ended,.

Fernand and Lea were both officers in the resistance in Belgium. All the members of Fernand's network, with the exception of one of his workers who had disobeyed him and had been caught, were saved. All the Jewish families who had been protected in their home were saved. Lea and Fernand are honored in Yad Vashem among the "Righteous of the Nations".

"I have often wondered how Jeanne's mother and father could have been so brave. How could they take such risks even though they had four small children? It was their faith in God. As descendants of the Huguenots, they already understood oppression, the necessity to flee for one's life, and to never compromise. They knew that the Jews are the chosen people of God and that, being Christians, they had to stand with them. They knew they must resist the forces of evil at all costs, even their lives, if need be.

Photo by permission of Yad Vashem
Raoul Wallenberg

Raoul Wallenberg

It is written in the Talmud that when someone saves one life it is as if he saved the whole world. This was exemplified in the life of Raoul Wallenberg.

While living in Palestine and working for a Dutch bank in Haifa in the 1930s, Wallenberg began to meet Jewish refugees arriving from Europe. He heard of the horrors of their suffering and the persecutions Jews were experiencing throughout Europe.

Wallenberg returned to his native Sweden and was eventually sent to Hungary to work as an attaché for the Swedish Embassy. He was given a special assignment to save Jewish lives. When he accepted the position, Wallenberg wanted permission to act without having to be accountable to the ambassador or anyone for the methods he would use. This unorthodox request was taken all the way to the prime minister and the king of Sweden. Wallenberg was given carte blanche to do whatever he deemed necessary to save Jewish lives.

From March to June of 1944, four-hundred thousand Hungarian Jews were deported to death camps under the supervision of Adolf Eichmann. In July of 1944, two-hundred-thirty thousand more Jews were scheduled to be taken and murdered. This would mean the end of Hungary's Jewish population and the fulfillment of Hitler's Final Solution for the country.

Wallenberg arrived in Budapest that July. He first rented rooms in a building near the Swedish Embassy and put signs on the doors calling the rooms the "Swedish Library." These facilities became hiding places for Jews. He then began mass-producing Swedish passports to give diplomatic protection to Jewish people assigned to be sent to the death camps. He entered lines of refugees waiting to board deportation trains and gave out the passports. Wallenberg would then yell and scream at the SS officers guarding the trains, demanding that the SS release the passport recipients because these people were under diplomatic protection by the neutral Swedish government. If they would not do so, Wallenberg would continue to shout and scream threats at the SS, which eventually would result in the release of the Jews. He even went into the trains, gave out passports, and then demanded the release of the pass holders before they could be taken to concentration camps. Many Jews were rescued. Wallenberg's influence spread to other embassies, causing other diplomats in Budapest to hide Jews.

It is estimated that Raoul Wallenberg saved as many as 100,000 Jews.

When he was asked by Swedes working with him in the embassy why he would take such risks, Wallenberg replied, "To me, there's no other choice. I've accepted this assignment, and I could never return to Stockholm without the knowledge that I had done everything within human power to save as many Jews as possible."

Wallenberg never returned to Sweden. The facts concerning his death are vague. The consensus is that he died in one of Stalin's gulags. But the one absolute about Raoul Wallenberg's life is that it was indeed a triumph of courage.

Photo by permission of Yad Vashem
Sophie and Hans Scholl, Christof Probst

Sophie and Hans Scholl

"Nothing is so unworthy of a civilized nation as allowing itself to be 'governed' without opposition by an irresponsible clique that has yielded to base instinct. It is certain that today every honest German is ashamed of his government. Who among us has any conception of the dimensions of shame that will befall us and our children when one day the veil has fallen from our eyes and the most horrible of crimes—crimes that infinitely out distance every human measure—reach the light of day?

"The day of reckoning has come—the reckoning of German youth with the most abominable tyrant our people have ever been forced to endure. We grew up in a state in which all free expression of opinion is ruthlessly suppressed. The Hitler Youth, the SA, the SS, have tried to regiment us in the most promising years of our lives. For us there is but one slogan: Fight against the party!

"The name of Germany is dishonored for all time if German youth do not finally rise, take revenge, smash their tormentors. Students! The German people look to us!" [2]

These words cost Sophie Scholl, her brother Hans, and their friend Christoph Probst their lives.

From 1939 to 1941, Hans Scholl, while a medic in the German army serving in Russia, witnessed mass murders of Jews committed by the SS and SA. In Poland, he witnessed the cruel slaughter of Jews in the Warsaw ghetto. Returning to Germany to study medicine at the University of Munich in 1942, Hans Scholl formed the White Rose resistance organization. He worked with six other students and a professor. Sophie eventually joined the organization. Their activities were based on nonviolent resistance. The group wrote and distributed six brochures decrying the evils of National Socialism. They painted sayings on walls, such as "Hitler: Mass Murderer," and they crossed out swastikas.

Robert Scholl, the father of Sophie and Hans, had been the mayor of Forchtenburg, Germany. He was imprisoned for saying, "This Hitler is God's scourge on mankind, and if this war doesn't end soon, the Russians will be sitting in Berlin." As an evangelical Christian, Scholl felt that he could not remain true to his faith and support Hitler's regime. At that time, Sophie was in the Hitler Youth, but through the example of her father's bravery, Sophie became critical of National Socialism.

Sophie worked for a while in Ulm as a kindergarten teacher and then came to Munich in 1942 to study biology and philosophy at the university. Leaving school, Sophie worked as a nursery school attendant and became increasingly involved in her brother's work in the resistance.

While distributing the sixth and last leaflet, Hans and Sophie were observed placing the papers in a building at the University of Munich by a member of the Nazi party. They were arrested before they could leave the building. Given a hasty trial by a vicious judge, Sophie, Hans, and Christoph Probst were sentenced to execution by guillotine. The execution was carried out two hours after the trial had ended.

Else Gebel, who shared a cell with Sophie, recorded Sophie's last words on the day of her trial and execution: "It is such a splendid day, and I have to go. But how many have to die on the battlefield on such days, how many young, promising lives? What does my death matter if by our acts thousands are warned and alerted?"

Sophie was twenty-one. Hans was twenty-four. They were so young, and their lives were so promising. Yet their sacrifice was not in vain. Many German youths were reached with their message. But these two have left behind an even greater legacy. Through them, we have seen what it means to be a true Christian and a righteous person in the face of evil and oppression.

Only a few of the stories of the brave men and women of the resistance have been presented in this discourse. They must be remembered. And we must be prepared to stand for right, as they did.

This is the message of the resistance, the righteous of the nations. And this message wasn't important for their time alone. It is for us today. May their lives challenge each one of us to be as they were, should such an unimaginable tragedy happen again. Most people remained silent and wouldn't speak out against the evils. They are forgotten. But the ones who stood for justice, though they were considered criminals by their oppressors, are today acknowledged as having taken the right decision. May the Lord prepare our hearts should we need to take a similar stand. And may God grant us grace to stand now, when anti-Semitism is growing and the world is rising up against Israel.

1. Smith, Martha J.: *Voices of the Resistance,* *a musical drama.* Copyright: 2008.

2. Scholl, Hans: Pamphlet, White Rose Resistance Organization, 1943.

CHAPTER 7

The Church: An Esther for a Time Like This

One evening in Oslo, my husband, Haakon, and I were attending a meeting of a Zionist group called With Israel for Peace (Med Israel for Fred). The speaker was Sagi Karni, the charge d'affaires of the Israeli Embassy in Norway. It was Purim time (the feast of Esther), and there were several Christians among the Jews in the audience. Gazing around the room with a very serious look on his face, Karni said, "You Christians are our Esther for this time in history." These words struck us like a lightning bolt. It was a commissioning, just as Mordechai had given his niece, Hadassah, who had become Esther, the queen of Persia. As a result of Mordechai's words, Esther saved the lives of her people.

The goal of anti-Semitism is always the same, whether it is embraced by Pharoah, Haman, the Philistines, Hitler, or Hamas. That aim is to destroy Israel and the Jewish people. We have a choice before us in this time of ever-increasing hate against the Jewish people. We can be silent to save our reputations. Or we can take a stand as Esther did and as Corrie Ten Boom, Raoul Wallenberg, and the other brave souls in the resistance did, in risking their lives to save Jews during World War II.

Why should the church support the Jews?

God is working by the power of the Holy Spirit throughout the world to prompt Gentile believers in the Jewish Messiah, Jesus, to love and stand with Israel and the Jewish people in the Diaspora.

One Sunday in August of 2011, I was preaching in an evangelical temple in the Cevenne mountains of France. There were, at most, about thirty people on hand. My sermon was on anti-Semitism in France and the Gentile believers' responsibility to stand with Israel and the Jews. A woman named Sabine, whom I had known for years, was in attendance. Sabine approached me after the service and said that the Lord was speaking to her during the sermon. The Holy Spirit had laid it on her heart to arrange a conference in her church in Avignon. She asked for prayer for the matter.

Several months later I received a call from another friend in France saying that Sabine had set up the first-ever Israel conference in her church. A visiting speaker from Israel deeply touched the hearts of the believers in attendance. Apparently, a vision was implanted in the congregants concerning the attitude of French believers toward the nation of Israel.

But why should the church support the Jews and Israel? To answer that question thoroughly, it is necessary to examine the relationship of the Gentile church to the Jews in several areas.

First of all, as Christians, we must be committed to the veracity of the Word of God. The Bible clearly shows that the Jewish people, the descendants of Abraham, Isaac, and Jacob, are God's chosen people. God said that He would bless those who bless them and curse those who curse them. He said that all nations would be blessed through them. God said that he would be a friend to their friends and an enemy to their enemies. So it would behoove us to stand with the Jewish people.

Secondly, aside from the benefits God bestows for loving and supporting the Jews and Israel, there is a requirement to choose sides. We cannot sit back in apathy and "play it safe" at a time like this. The 700 Club news show recently presented a report on "Belgistan" or Belgium, which is being taken over by Islam. The leader of "Shariah4Belgium,"

Abu Imran, was interviewed. He clearly stated that the goal of his organization was to gain full control over Belgium and that this plan was being implemented through population growth. The report noted that 40 percent of the babies born in hospitals in Brussels were named Mohammad. (It is important to note that Brussels is the capital of the European Union.) In a celebration of the Norseman's Association's 100th anniversary, Jonas Gahr Støre, the Norwegian Foreign Minister, said that 50% of the babies born in Oslo in that year were named Mohamed, Ali or other Muslim names. This pattern is being repeated throughout Europe.

Imran said that a country cannot be Islamic without shariah law. He said that Muslims who consider themselves "democratic Muslims" and don't believe in shariah are not Muslims. The two cannot exist together. Imran declared that democracy and Islam are opposites. Islam is ruled by "Allah's" laws, while democracy, as Abraham Lincoln wrote in the Gettysburg Address, is "of the people, by the people and for the people." Imran said that Islam and shariah are synonymous and that one cannot exist without the other.

Dutch author, Sam Van Roy, who recently co-authored and edited the book *Islam: Critical Essays on a Political Religion*[1], denounces Islam as fascist and sees a bleak future for Europe. He feels it is inevitable that Islam will dominate Europe. Because of the post-Christian society in Europe, there is no faith-basis to counteract Islam's bid for dominance. In past history, the Christian faith has always been the bulwark against Islam's advances. This was evident in history from Charles Martel to Le Cid and the conquests of Vienna and Eastern Europe. Democracy's downfall will be a result of the freedom democratic countries give to Islamo-fascism while rejecting their own Christian heritage.

Seeing the threat that Islam poses to the Jews and all of Western society, Christians, as friends of the Jews and as people who understand the Biblical mandate for the existence of the nation of Israel, must take a stand for God's chosen ones. This stand is not for them alone, but for the preservation of democracy and Western society.

Those appointed to destruction

As Proverbs 31 states, we are called to speak out for those appointed to destruction. To speak out for those who cannot speak out for themselves. How can Israel speak out for herself when world media seem to have decided to present only a biased, one-sided, negative view of Israel? We, the Gentile Christians, are among the minority willing to support Israel's struggle for survival.

There are many ways in which we can make the truth about Israel known. But first and foremost, we must overcome the fear of man. Standing up for Israel is not a popular thing to do today. My dear Christian friend, Bjørg Lillereiten was a tiny woman, but a great warrior for Israel. She had a prayer group that met every week to pray for Israel. She organized the first and only "messianic" church in Oslo, called Beit Immanuel. We had the privilege of working with Bjørg on many Israel-related projects: concerts, conferences, and television programs. She traveled to Israel more than forty times to show her solidarity. For many years, wherever she went, Bjørg wore earrings and a necklace with the Star of David. Many times, she was verbally attacked and threatened for openly wearing this symbol of Israel. But Bjørg would not back down. Nor would she take off her earrings and necklace.

There are many ways in which we may show our solidarity with the Jewish people and the nation of Israel. Every voice is needed.

Judgment of the nations

In explaining the judgment of the world, Jesus said the criterion that He will use to evaluate the nations will be the treatment they have given to His brethren.

> When the Son of Man comes in his glory and all the angels with him, he will sit on his throne in heavenly glory. All the nations will be gathered before him, and he will separate the people one from another as a shepherd separates the sheep from the goats. He will put the sheep on his right and the goats on his left. Then the King will say to those on his right, "Come, you who are blessed by my Father; take you inheritance, the

kingdom prepared for you since the creation of the world. For I was hungry and you gave me something to eat, I was thirsty and you gave me something to drink, I was a stranger and you invited me in, I needed clothes and you clothed me, I was sick and you looked after me, I was in prison and you came to visit me." Then the righteous will answer him, "Lord, when did we see you hungry and feed you, or thirsty and give you something to drink? When did we see you a stranger and invite you in, or needing clothes and clothe you? When did we see you sick or in prison and visit you?" The King will reply, "I tell you the truth, whatever you did for one of the least of these, my brethren, you did for me."
—Matt. 25:31–40 NIV [2]

We, the Gentile church, as a result of thorough brainwashing through replacement theology, have supposed that this passage was referring exclusively to us. Nothing could be further from the truth. The reason for God's judgment on the nations is clearly spelled out in the book of Joel:

I will gather all nations and bring them down to the valley of Jehosaphat. Then I will enter into judgment with them there on behalf of my people, and my inheritance, Israel, whom they have scattered among the nations and they have divided up my land. Joel 3:2, NAS [3]

These passages are interrelated. Both refer to judgment of the nations. They also refer to the physical brethren of Jesus, the Jewish people.

Therefore, what should be our response as believers? We are to clothe the naked, visit the sick and suffering, and aid those in distress, according to Jesus' words. These judgment passages indicate that a choice must be made, both on the national and individual levels. The passage in Joel says that those who oppose Israel's right to exist, those who would destroy her, will themselves be destroyed.

A twofold mandate is presented in these passages: 1) We are to care for the Jewish people and Israel. And 2) we are to stand with Israel against those who seek her annihilation.

Obedience in these areas is a determining factor not only in our own assessment as believers. There is a reciprocal effect on the position of the nations with the Lord. The nations are deemed righteous (the sheep) or unrighteous (the goats) in accordance with their treatment of the Jewish people. Our choice as believers in this matter has much to say in the final assessment of the nations before the judgment seat of Christ.

The Church's record of anti-Semitism

The last consideration as to why it is so important that Christians stand with the Jewish people regards the church's history of anti-Semitism. Christian anti-Semitism has been the source of horrific suffering for innocent Jewish people over the centuries. In addition, it has brought great dishonor to the name of our Savior. Both the Nicean and Lateren Councils passed judgments and made statements against the Jews which led to attacks and pogroms through the centuries: the blood-libel hoax of the Middle Ages; the Spanish and Portuguese inquisitions; the pogroms throughout Christian Europe in which multitudes of Jews died for being "Christ killers"; the hoax of The Protocols of the Elders of Zion 4; the silence of Christians during the Holocaust because of anti-Semitic attitudes and/or pastoral guidance to "submit to government authorities"; the numerous church denominations that have rejected Israel's right to defend herself and have withdrawn their financial support in favor of the Palestinians. All of these acts against the Jewish people over the centuries have been perpetrated in "Christian" countries, and most were done in the name of Christ. This is an indictment against the the nations and the church. In January of 2012, a prophetic word was given to a pastor in England regarding England's treatment of the Jews. The same word was given to a congregation in Cambridgeshire in 1992. The word was this:

> The Lord would use you to bring together the pastors, Christian leaders, and Christians of this nation in a time of national repentance for the evils Great Britain has done to the Jews and the nation of Israel. England shut the doors of

Palestine to Jews seeking to flee Hitler's inferno. When the war was over and the camps were emptied, England again barred the doors of Palestine to Jews. Boats overflowing with refugees were stopped off the coast of Palestine, and Jews were prevented from entering the land. The British then directed refugee ships to Cyprus where the passengers, Jews coming from concentration camps, were forced into detention camps very similar to the ones they had just left—high fences and barbed wire. In 1948, when it was decided that Israel should be established as a nation, the British, before leaving Palestine, armed the Arabs while refusing to allow Jews to have weapons to protect themselves from their unfriendly neighbors.

It is time for the church of this nation, as a whole, to gather and ask forgiveness for the sins committed by the United Kingdom against the Jewish people. Call the leaders, call all the people of God together, and humble yourselves and ask forgiveness.

Because of these sins against the Jews, your nation came under a curse in 1948. The U.K. which once had half of the landmass of the earth, lost almost all of its territory within a few years. India, many nations of Africa, the Pacific, and Latin America were all gone within a few decades. There is a building near this church here which was formerly an Anglican Church, Church of England. It is now a mosque. The Lord says that repentance, which begins with the people of God, must take place for the healing of this land, or this former church which is now a mosque will serve as a symbol of the destiny of England.

Great Britain is not the only nation with a dark past regarding treatment of the Jews. The United States closed her ports to Jews trying to escape Hitler's inferno. At the Evian Conference in France in 1938 when Hitler offered to release the Jews to live in other nations of the world, only the Dominican Republic would take even a few of the refugees.

God is looking for an Esther for a time like this, one willing to confront the evils that threaten the Jews. The church does indeed have a record of offenses against the Jews that we must acknowledge. Until we do so and until we align ourselves on the side of the Jewish people and Israel, we will never experience the fullness of God's inheritance. We, the body of Christ, must be willing to acknowledge the crimes committed against the Jews by the church and by our nations. By repenting and taking our stand with the chosen people of God, we may see our nations turn from a goat herd into a sheepfold.

1. Van Roy, Sam & Van Roy, Wim: *Islam: Critical Essays on a Political Religion* (Dutch: *De Islam: Kritische Essays over een Politieke Religie.*) Boekhandel de Zondyloed, Mechelen, Holland, 2010.

2. *The Holy Bible: New International Version*

3. *The Holy Bible: New American Standard Version*

4. *The Protocols of the Learned Elders of Zion,* trans. from Russian, Victor E. Mardsen. Rivercrest Publishing, Austin, Tex., 1934, reprint: 2011.

CHAPTER 8

The Sheep and the Goats

What would Jesus do? Jesus said that His criteria in judging whether nations are sheep or goats will be this: inasmuch as you have done this unto these my brethren, you have done it unto me. Who are Jesus' brethren? Jesus is a Jew. The Bible says He came to his own, the Jewish people. He was circumcised. He kept all the Jewish festivals. He preached in the synagogues. Jesus is a Jew! What a surprise for many Gentile Christians who have thought of Jesus as a blond-haired, blue-eyed Scandinavian!

The treatment of His brethren by the Gentile nations is the basis on which Jesus will decide the fate of the countries of the world. It is, therefore, important for the welfare of our nations and for our own lives that we take a stand with the Jewish people and Israel.

The Jewish people, as a whole, are hard-working and resourceful. Education is a high priority in many Jewish families. From the Jewish people have come leaders of corporations, professors, scientists, musicians, artists, writers, researchers and others in leadership positions in society. This being the case, many would ask themselves, "Why should a people with such a high success rate need my help?"

The world Jewish population as of 2010 was at approximately 13.3 million Jews world-wide with 8.3 million living in the Diaspora and 4.9 million living in Israel. [1] The Jewish people represent a small segment of world population. Centuries of persecution have propagated stereo-types and prejudices toward Jews. Current trends of growing anti-Semitism world-wide present threats to the welfare of the Jewish Diaspora and to the continued existence of the Jewish state, Israel. Various factors surrounding the growing trends of hatred against the Jewish people will be discussed in more depth in later chapters.

The question remains: What can the Church do to help Israel and the Diaspora? Jesus said that we are to feed, clothe, visit, and care for the poor of His people. Scripture further says that we are to speak out for those who cannot speak for themselves. We are to pray for the peace of Jerusalem and to be a blessing to Israel.

We must care about the welfare of the Jewish people and Israel. To do so, it is important that we understand the opposition and threats Israel faces. A major obstacle for the church in understanding their role toward the Jews is "replacement theology," which has weakened the church in its support of the state of Israel. This misconception must be corrected. Believers must then be informed about Islamic threats against Israel. Neo-Nazi and white extremist groups pose a serious danger to Jews throughout the Diaspora. Media propaganda against Israel is another source of anti-Semitism, as it feeds upon existing anti-Jewish stereotypes. The current trends of political correctness would seek to impose a negative view of Israel and the Jews as being the "correct way to perceive the matter." These are the major pressures Israel and the Diaspora face. For Christians to make an effective stand against these concepts, it is necessary to examine their roots and development. Information is power, whether it be on the negative side or on the side of those who would seek to refute error.

1. World Jewish Population Statistics, *Jewish Virtual Library*, 2010.

CHAPTER 9

Replacement Theology: A Doctrine from Hell

Satan has unfortunately found a successful tool to delegitimize the Jewish people in the eyes of the church. That is the doctrine of "replacement theology." This teaching espouses that God is finished with the Jewish people and that all His promises and election have been transferred to the church, meaning Gentile and Jewish believers in Jesus, the Messiah. Proponents of this doctrine maintain a concept of two Israels—a physical Israel, meaning the Jews, and a "spiritual Israel," meaning the church, mostly made up of Gentile believers. The biblical basis for replacement theology has come from manipulation of Scripture passages such as:

> A man is not a Jew if he is only one outwardly, nor is circumcision merely outward and physical. No, a man is a Jew if he is one inwardly; and circumcision is circumcision of the heart, by the Spirit, not by the written code. Such a man's praise is not from men, but from God. [1]
> —Rom. 2:28–29 NIV

> Therefore, be sure that it is those who are of faith who are the sons of Abraham. [2]
> —Gal. 3:7 NAS

> And if you belong to Christ, then you are Abraham's descendants, heirs according to the promise. **3**
> —Gal. 3:29 NIV

It is important to remember that these verses were written primarily for Gentile believers, not Jews. There was a great debate at that time over the question of whether Gentiles could be saved. In the verses quoted above, Paul was reaffirming the relationship between Gentile Christians and God, not negating the eternal covenant the Jewish people share with God because of their fathers, Abraham, Isaac and Jacob.

There was also an argument over whether Gentile converts needed to be circumcised. Paul dealt with that issue by arguing that these converts had circumcised hearts and therefore did not need a physical procedure to have a right standing with God. However, when Paul was preparing Timothy for ministry, who was the son of a Jewish woman, he circumcised him. Scripture seems to indicate that the Jewish apostles and Jewish members of the early church maintained elements of their Jewish tradition. When the apostles met to decide whether or not Gentile believers should have to fulfill the law, they stipulated only that they should not eat meats that were strangled, bloody or offered to idols and that they should abstain from fornication. This would seem to imply that the Jewish contingency within the church continued to employ kosher food practices but that Gentiles were exempt from these traditions, as they were unfamiliar with them.

Proponents of replacement theology say that when God judged the Jews and they were sent into exile, He forever rejected them and replaced them with the church. However, the Bible in both testaments clearly indicates an eternal relationship between God and the Jewish people.

> "I will restore the captivity of my people Israel. They will rebuild the ruined cities and live in them. They will also plant vineyards and drink their wine. And make gardens and eat their fruit. I will also plant them on their land and they will

not again be rooted out from their land which I have given
them," says the Lord your God. [4]
—Amos 9:14–15 NAS

God declares that He has an eternal relationship and covenant with
the Jewish people. He will return them to their land and they will
not be removed again, according to Amos 9. This Scripture can in no
way refer to the Gentile church. It is a literal reference to the Jewish
people.

Yes, there is a requirement that we come to faith in Jesus and
repentance from sin to be in a right relationship with God, but the
Jewish people's restoration to the land of Israel was not contingent on
their repentance or their faith in Jesus. It was a sovereign decision of
the Most High God.

Return, O Israel, to the Lord your God. You have stumbled
because of your iniquity. Take words with you and return to
the Lord. Say to Him, "Take away all iniquity and receive us
graciously, that we may present the fruit of our lips." ... I will
heal your apostasy. I will love them freely. For my anger has
turned away from them. [5]
—Hos. 14:1–2, 4 NAS

God is calling Israel and all of humanity to faith in Jesus and to
repentance. He desires to have a relationship with all of humanity
through faith in His Son. But this does not negate the eternal covenant
God made with the people of Israel.

In Romans 11, Paul refuted replacement theology, which may have
begun to infect the church even in the early stages of its development.
Writing to the church of Rome, he rejected the basic tenets of the
heresy that Israel had been rejected for all eternity and defended the
position of his people and their eternal covenant with God.

God has not rejected His people, has He? May it never be!
For I, too, am an Israelite, a descendant of Abraham, of the

tribe of Benjamin. God has not rejected His people whom He foreknew. [6]
—Rom. 11:1–2 NAS

Paul offers the truth about our relationship with the Jewish people and about the fallacy of replacement theology:

> If the first piece of dough is holy, the lump is also; and if the root is holy, the branches are too. But if some of the branches are broken off, and you, being a wild olive, were grafted in among them and became partaker with them of the rich root of the olive tree, do not be arrogant toward the branches; but if you are arrogant, remember that it is not you who supports the root, but the root supports you. [7]
> —Rom. 11:16–18 NAS

Oh, the arrogance of the Gentile church through the ages to presume that it had replaced the Jewish people and that God's eternal covenant with the Jews had been negated. Shame on us!

We haven't replaced the Jewish people or the nation of Israel. On the contrary, we have become part of them! It is important to remember that the early church was mostly Jewish and that the Scriptures manipulated to support the heretical doctrine of replacement theology were primarily written to non-Jews outside of Israel to clarify that they could be saved, too.

It is clear from the eleventh chapter of Romans that "replacement theology," or the "spiritual Israel" teaching, was another strategy from hell sent against the Jewish people. This teaching left its traces in the doctrines of the Roman Catholic Church, the Orthodox Church, Martin Luther's teachings, and the teachings of the Protestant reformists. "Replacement theology" coupled with rumors and false accusations against Jews, served the Gentile church as a justification to commit pogroms and to discriminate against Jews throughout the past two millennia. But how did this doctrine gain such a stronghold in Christian teaching?

1. *The Holy Bible: New International Version*
2. *The Holy Bible: New American Standard Version*
3. *The Holy Bible: New International Version*
4. *The Holy Bible: New American Standard Version*
5. *The Holy Bible: New American Standard Version*
6. *The Holy Bible: New American Standard Version*
7. *The Holy Bible: New American Standard Version*

CHAPTER 10

Constantine:
The Roots of Replacement
Theology and its Consequences

Two Jewish women were recently visiting a museum in New York City where they viewed a famous painting entitled "Jesus, the Jew." A Christian woman wearing a cross saw the name of the painting and angrily said, "Jesus wasn't a Jew. How dare they say that?" The two secular Jewish women then felt responsible to defend Jesus' Jewish roots to the Christian woman. What a paradox!

This true story is representative of the misconception that much of the church has had over the centuries. How did Christians get the idea that Jesus was a blond-haired, blue-eyed Scandinavian?

Fortunately, there is a move of the Holy Spirit taking place worldwide in which, little by little, the Gentile church is beginning to realize that our Savior, Jesus, whom we love and serve, is indeed a Jew. At the same time, the Lord is calling Gentile Christians to take a stand alongside our Jewish brothers and the nation of Israel. The Gentile church is returning home to her roots.

But how did the church go from being a very Jewish entity to become the source of persecution and great suffering for the Jews for so many centuries? Many factors contributed to this debacle, but some influences have played a central role. They are: 1) Constantine's edict of tolerance; 2) assimilation of the church into the Roman empire as the state religion; 3) removal of everything "Jewish" from the Christian faith; 4) demonization of the Jews; and 5) establishment of a hierarchical structure in the church patterned after the Roman governmental structure.

It is important that we examine the breach that developed between the structure of the early church and the assimilation process forced upon the church by the Roman government.

The early church's divorce from its Jewish roots

A clear pattern was established in the early church in which the leadership was, as Jesus put it, "the servant of all." Apostles, prophets, evangelists, pastors, and teachers were laying down their lives for the saints, or laity. They knew very well that their function was to "equip the saints for the work of the ministry", even as Jesus had done with his disciples. Paul spent countless hours instructing and preparing the leaders throughout the Diaspora to guard the church after he would depart. He knew clearly that wolves would arise among the leaders who would speak perversely "to draw away the disciples after them" (Acts 20:30).

The "Jewish" early church took special steps to be sure that its Jewish roots would be preserved. Although Gentile believers were required only to abstain from foods with blood and from strangled animals and food offered to idols and to avoid sexual immorality, Jewish believers maintained their heritage of the law out of respect for God, not as a means of attaining salvation. When Paul returned to Jerusalem (Acts 20:16), he did so with all haste to be there for the feast of Shavuot. Shavuot, or Pentecost, according to the Greek, was the day when Moses was said to have received the Torah. It is also the day when the believers of Jerusalem received the Holy Spirit with evidence of speaking in tongues. All those present heard what the disciples were saying in their own languages, even though they were visiting Jerusalem from many different nations.

When Paul arrived in Jerusalem, he was told that rumors had spread about him, accusing him of "teaching all the Jews who are among the

Gentiles to forsake Moses, telling them not to circumcise their children, nor to walk according to the customs" (Acts 21:21). Jewish believers in the early church continued to practice Jewish traditions to some degree. Examination of Paul's life as representative of early church attitudes and practices shows a consistent relationship between Jewish law and tradition and his service to the Lord. Paul, according to Acts 18:18 kept a Nazarite vow. After the vow was completed, he had his hair cut as was stipulated in Numbers 6:18. (The parents of Samson made a Nazarite vow for their son, as a form of separation to the Lord.) It appears that the early church set events in their lives in relation to the Jewish holy days. For example, in Acts 20:16, Paul hurried to try to reach Jerusalem by Pentecost. In 1 Cor. 16:8, Paul said he would remain in Ephesus until Pentecost. So it would seem that early church believers planned the events of their lives according to the Jewish feasts, not according to the Roman calendar. Jewish tradition was an important factor in the every day life of the early church, especially in Israel.

In AD 70, with the destruction of the Temple in Jerusalem, many Jewish people were slaughtered by the Romans or driven out of the land and scattered throughout the nations. Many were taken as slaves to Rome. The assimilation process would be completed and every vestige of the Jewish roots of the church would be removed. The treasures of the Temple and the enslavement of the Jewish people at the time of the Temple's destruction can still be seen engraved on the arch of the Emperor Titus which is in the ancient Roman forum in Rome.

However, the period from AD 33 to AD 311 was a time of exponential growth in the church. It was also a time of great suffering for the body of Jesus. Eusebius in his *Ecclesiastical History* reported torture and martyrdom in much of the church. The Romans destroyed churches and houses of prayer. Christians were fed to the lions, tied to poles and set on fire to light the streets of Rome and the Circus Maximus, many were crucified as the Lord Jesus was, and others were subjected to numerous other forms of torture and execution. [1]

The worst persecution took place under the Emperor Diocletian (AD 284-305). For twenty years, Diocletian respected the Edict of Toleration toward the Christians that had been issued by Gallienus.

Most of Diocletian's family and court had become believers, although he remained a pagan. In AD 304, Diocletian abandoned all restraint and "destroyed churches, burned Bibles, deprived Christians of all privileges and ordered their execution as sacrifices to pagan gods" But the death throes to end persecution by the Roman Empire were at hand, an indication of the end to the official state persecution of the church. However, a more insidious threat followed that might be likened to the political correctness being forced on the body of Christ today. That threat was assimilation to the Roman system.

The edict of tolerance

Galerius, emperor from 305 to 311, continued the persecution of the Christians which had been instigated by Diocletian. However, when he became sick with a terrible disease, which he felt had been inflicted on him by the Christian God, he relented and issued an edict of tolerance before his death. In 313, Constantine met his brother-in-law and co-regent, Licinius, in Milan. There the two enacted a further order of tolerance. Persecution continued in isolated parts of the Roman Empire following this final edict, but generally peace had come to the church.

Until 311, Christianity was intrinsically Jewish. The Messiah was Jewish. The apostles were Jews. Peter, James, John, Andrew—all were Jewish. The first believers were Jews. The church was birthed in the Jewish homeland of Israel. The feast days of the Jewish faith were an important part of the lives of the first Christians.

But with the assimilation of the church into the Roman Empire under the Emperor Constantine, every element of "Jewishness" was extracted from the body of the Messiah.

The First Council of Nicaea

In the First Council of Nicaea, AD 325, it was decided that all trappings of Jewish custom, whether biblical or not, were to be removed from the church. Constantine echoed the sentiments of the council in a letter, referring to the separation of the Passover date from the date of Easter and saying "it appeared an unworthy thing that in the celebration of this most holy feast we should follow the practice of the Jews, who have impiously defiled their hands with enormous sin, and are, therefore, deservedly afflicted with blindness of soul ... Let us then have nothing in common with the detestable Jewish crowd; for we have received from our Savior a different way" [2]

"The Epistle of the Emperor Constantine," reporting on the decisions of the Nicene Council, says: "It was, in the first place, declared improper to follow the custom of the Jews in the celebration of this holy festival, because their hands having been stained with crime, the minds of these wretched men are necessarily blinded ... Let us, then, have nothing in common with the Jews, who are our adversaries ... Let us ... studiously avoid all contact with that evil way ... For how can they entertain right views on any point who, after having compassed the death of the Lord, being out of their minds, are guided not by sound reason, but by an unrestrained passion, wherever their innate madness carries them ... lest your pure minds should appear to share in the customs of a people so utterly depraved ... Therefore, this irregularity must be corrected, in order that we may no more have anything in common with those parricides and the murderers of our Lord ... no single point in common with the perjury of the Jews" [3]

It is clear from communications following the Council of Nicaea every effort was to be made to eliminate the Judeo roots of the Christian faith.

This made the way clear for the Romanization of the church as it was re-established after the customs and practices of Roman culture. The Roman pantheon of gods was replaced by the saints. Juno, one of the major goddesses of Roman mythology, was replaced by Mary, the mother of Jesus. Mary, or Miriam, her Jewish name, was no long the humble Jewish girl who had said, upon hearing that she should bear the Messiah, "My soul praises the Lord and my spirit rejoices in God, my savior. He has been mindful of the humble estate of his servant." (Luke 1:46-48) Now Mary was a goddess. Mary declared herself to need a savior and to be but a humble servant of God. But now, following the Council of Nicaea's decision, Mary was subsequently elevated to the status of a goddess and an intercessor between God and man. She unfortunately continues to be held by some as an equal to Jesus or God the Father.

During the assimilation process of the very Jewish church of Jesus, Constantine held true to his decision to rid the church of every trace of its Jewish heritage. Christianity would be a purely Roman state religion, The Scriptures say there is one intercessor between God and man, Jesus. But through the extra-biblical integration of Roman thought, there were many intercessors between God and man: the son and his mother, Mary, and the saints, who had replaced the pantheon of Roman gods.

It that wasn't tragic enough, Mary was given titles derived from pagan deities. The goddess Juno was called *regina*, meaning queen. This same title was given to the deified Mary. Another title given Mary under the Roman church was *regina coeli,* or *queen of heaven*. This term was applied in antiquity to goddesses in many nations, including Anat, a northwestern Semitic goddess who was a lover of Baal and was associated with war; Isis in Egypt; Innana, a Sumerian fertility goddess; Astarte, a Mesapotamian goddess; Hera, a Greek goddess; Asherah, a Semitic mother goddess, and Frigg, a Nordic goddess.

Even though the Ten Commandments forbid making idols of any kind, statues, such as were found in Roman temples, were now erected in honor of Mary and the saints throughout the churches of the Roman Empire. The commandment against idolatry was of no avail:

"Thou shall not make unto thee any graven image of anything in the heaven above, the earth beneath and the waters under the earth. Thou shalt not bow down to them and serve them" Ex. 20:4-5, KJV. [4]

Having said this, it is important to mention that there are many wonderful believers in the Roman Catholic Church. This body has valiantly stood against the tides of humanism and iniquity that are spreading throughout the earth. But it would behoove the Church of Rome to examine its doctrine against Biblical truth and to allow the Lord to correct all error that has crept in over the centuries. All denominations of the Christian faith need to do so. The only way to judge the validity of doctrine is to test it against the Word of God, the Bible. That is why it is so important to expose the causes of the church's departure from its Jewish roots and its shift from Biblical truth.

The Last Outpost of the Apostolic or Early Church

Dr. Robert Heidler, a prominent theologian and Bible teacher, presented a discourse on the life of Patrick (or St. Patrick, as the Roman Catholic Church would later call him) the apostle to the nation of Ireland. Patrick, born in A.D. 389, was a Roman Britain who grew up in a Christian family. As a young man, Patrick traveled to pagan Ireland to live, where he had a dramatic encounter with God. He returned to England for some years and then came back to then-pagan Ireland where God used him to birth the Celtic church. Heidler described the Celtic church as the "last outpost of apostolic Christianity" after the model of the early church. According to the pattern of the Lord Jesus and the apostles, Patrick healed the sick; raised 33 dead people back to life; cast out demons; and trained and appointed apostles, among whom were (Brigid (a woman), Columba, Brenden and Comgall. Patrick and his apostolic colleagues established evangelistic centers; bringing revival to the nation of Ireland, Scotland, Wales and the surrounding islands.

The church Patrick established was not Roman Catholic, as the first Roman Catholic missionaries did not come to Ireland until 200 years after Patrick's time. Also, the model of the Celtic church established by Patrick differed greatly from the church of Rome..

- They didn't believe in purgatory.
- They didn't honor the Pope.
- They did honor Mary but didn't pray to her.
- The priests and monks in the Celtic Church married and had children.
- The Celtic Church baptized converts by immersion.
- They observed Christian Passover, not Roman Easter.
- They observed the sabbath, resting on the seventh day (Saturday) and worshipped on the first day of the week (Sunday).
- They strongly emphasized equipping the saints for the work of the ministry.
- They began their days at sunset as the Hebrews did, with a day beginning and ending from sunset to sunset.

- They developed evangelistic centers to reach the world, not monasteries to keep the world out.
- 24 hour a day continuous prayer and praise was implemented, after the model of the Temple in Jerusalem.

How could the Celtic church be so much like the early church as it existed in the book of Acts?

According to Heidler's research, Patrick's forefathers were Jewish believers in Jesus. They had fled Israel around A.D. 70 during the Roman siege of Jerusalem under Titus and Vespasian and settled in Roman Britain. They carried with them the traditions and practices of the apostles, as received from the Lord Jesus, himself.

200 years after Patrick, as the Catholic church took control of the religious life of the people of Britain, great pressure was put on the Celtic church to become a part of the Roman church. The main issue of contention between the two regarded celebrating the Christian Passover versus Roman Easter.

According to Dr. Heidler, Julia Bolton Holloway, professor emeritus of Medieval studies at the University of Colorado stated that most legends concerning Patrick say he was of Jewish ancestry with his family having fled Israel from the Romans to resettle in Britain. . A much older manuscript based on even more ancient sources, "The Book of Leinster", pg. 353, vol. 4, A.D. 1160, refers to Patrick's Jewish roots and his family's flight to Britain from besieged Jerusalem in A.D. 70.

Nicolaitanism

There are very few statements in the Bible where it says that God hates something. But one of the things mentioned which God detests is the teaching of the Nicolaitans. There was a sect called the Nicolaitans in the time of the early church. Eusebius says this sect was short-lived and their influence inconsequential. However, for the point of this study, it is relevant to examine the word *Nicolaitan* rather than the sect. This word is a composite of the Greek word *nico,* which means *to conquer,* and *laitan,* the root word for *laity* or *lay people.* The picture described by this word is of a hierarchical structure in which one group rules over the other. This certainly describes the structure of the Roman government, in which the emperor, senators, equestrians, provincial governors, legion commanders, and other aristocrats were all-powerful and the emperor was heralded as a god after his death while the people were subservient to the leaders.

In the context of the church and aside from the heretical adoration of the saints and deification of Mary which was used to replace the Roman Pantheon of Gods, the Roman state implemented a new paradigm in the leadership model of the church. No longer was the emphasis on the priesthood of the believers, with the leadership—apostles, prophets, evangelists, pastors, and teachers—being facilitators to teach and equip believers for their role in ministry.

Under the original model, the entire church functioned to do the work of ministry. The leaders ministered to the laity to equip them while the laity functioned in ministry in the world outside the church. Stephen, who was a deacon, or lay minister, was noted for being filled with faith and the Holy Spirit (Acts 6:5). He had been prepared for ministry in accordance with the structural mandate found in Ephesians 4, which says that those in the offices of apostle, prophet, evangelist, pastor, and teacher were appointed for the sole purpose of serving the laity. Paul wrote in Ephesians 4 that leaders were to "equip the saints for the work of the ministry." The *saints* referred to those not in the offices of apostle, prophet, evangelist, pastor, and teacher. Therefore the laity are to do the work of ministry. The leader's ministry is to equip them to do so.

This implies a student-teacher or athlete-trainer type of relationship. It is a system quite similar to the teacher-student relationship in a Jewish yeshiva, a teaching methodology which has evolved from the time of the patriarchs. In the Jewish educational system, students do not sit in silence as the teacher pontificates. Rather the students are taught to question the teacher and to try to propose answers that may be contrary to the teacher's theories. The Jewish model of Torah study has existed since the Torah was given. It was a methodology that worked well to prepare a priesthood of believers. The "yeshiva-style" paradigm prevailed up until the time of the church's schism from its Jewish roots.

Following the Church's assimilation into the role of being the Roman State Church, a new structure was established that followed the format of Roman government. As mentioned above, the Roman governmental hierarchy included emperor, governors, equestrians, senators, and local officials. Similarly, the church now had a pope, cardinals, archbishops, bishops and priests. While Jesus and his disciples dressed in the common clothing of their time and culture, the robes and dress of the clergy in the State Church of Rome were inspired by the magnificent robes of Roman emperors. The headdresses resembled crowns. A new monarchy was now in place. A hierarchy had been established that would rule over the laity even as the word "Nicolaitan" implies. The priesthood of believers had been abolished, and the laity were subservient to the clergy.

After this structure was imposed upon the church, there was no longer an egalitarian fellowship of believers, with each being equipped to minister by leaders trained to be "servants of all." Now a hierarchical structure was formed: priests, bishops, cardinals, archbishops, and the pope. The leaders were made responsible for the work of ministry, while the people, the laity, were made to serve the clergy. The laity was to be in absolute submission to the leaders' demands. This paradigm was in direct opposition to the model of discipleship Jesus employed with his followers and to the functional structure within the apostolic ministry of the early church.

For centuries, believers were forbidden to read the Bible (until the time of the Reformation). Clergy understood that if believers were allowed to read the Bible they would realize that they had been enslaved by this hierarchical system. Church leadership feared that the truth about the role of clergy would be revealed. This would weaken the Roman church's hold over the laity. The church could thereby lose the wealth it had accrued by dominating over the people. (In the Museum of the Desert in southern France, a repeated theme presented to explain the persecution of the Huguenot Christians was that the Catholic clergy feared the loss of power and wealth due to the enlightenment of the Huguenots who were avid Bible readers.) The Bible is a threat to the existence of this Nicolaitan system and is equally feared in every totalitarian system.

The Bible says that it is for freedom's sake that Christ has set us free. Believers who discover their rights and privileges in Jesus, the Jewish Messiah, can bring an end to the oppressive system. Clergy would be "dethroned". They would no longer be able to abuse the laity, for example, by requiring large amounts of money for indulgences to go to heaven. As the true role of leadership would emerge, the clergy would have to become servants to equip the laity, rather than task masters exploiting the body of Christ. God intended leaders to be servants, not oppressors. Should the truth about leadership's role become apparent, the positions of those abusing authority would be dissolved. The vast wealth of the church would be used to provide for the poor and hungry, as Jesus intended, instead of being used to build palaces and amass untold wealth for the clerical leaders.

A visit to the Vatican is an overwhelming experience: the magnificent buildings, the art treasures, and all the wealth the church possesses. I remember traveling through Italy and seeing poverty in many cities and towns. Touring the Vatican museum in Rome, where the church's riches are on display, I found the contrast shocking. Jesus never intended for this to be the case. On the contrary, He said that, after our own needs are met, we are to use the wealth He provides to feed the poor, clothe the naked, minister to those in want, and to preach the Gospel. But, again, the Roman paradigm of hierarchical control and wealth accumulation for a privileged class has prevailed.

This discussion is not meant to be a diatribe against the Roman church. The same scenario is played out in some Protestant and evangelical circles where pastors and leaders operate as potentates controlling the lives of their congregants. Manipulative suggestions are often made regarding the status of a member's walk with God if a member dares to question the pastor's authority. A favorite quote used to gain control of the people of God is "Touch not my anointed." As this is frequently quoted to force laity to mindlessly submit to abusive leadership, people who sincerely love God tolerate the oppression of their leaders as part of their "service to God." "The man of God can't be wrong."

There certainly are many wonderful, selfless leaders in the church who lay down their lives for the people of God. However, there have been frequent incidents of leaders from every church denomination who have taken advantage of their position and authority to misuse the laity. This is the Nicolaitan model—a ruler class and a conquered class. The Lord says in Revelations 2:6,

> Yet this you do have, that you hate the deeds of the Nicolaitans, which I also hate. NAS [5]

God hates the "Nicolaitan" precedent of control and exploitation, whether it appears in the Catholic, Pentecostal, Baptist, Methodist or Lutheran form.

It was never the Lord's intention to have his people subservient to a class system. But this system has prevailed to the present day, even in evangelical churches. In some churches, his royal highness, the pastor, controls all ministry and is threatened if laity try to raise up into their God-given callings. In such an environment, those beginning to come into using their spiritual gifts as God would raise them up to minister or those sensing the call of God on their lives will be quickly shut down because they pose a threat to the leader's position of supremacy.

A case in point: a friend named Hans was active in a Pentecostal church. He began to seek the Lord about the call he had received which was to pray for healing for the sick. God was using him in a mighty way to bring healing to many people. When the pastor of his church found out, he became jealous. He closed down Hans' ministry and spread rumors that he was operating a sect. In recent years, another friend of mine, who also prayed for the sick, was in this same church. This same pastor responded in the same way to this dear brother. This is just one isolated incident, but it is indicative of the Nicolaitan mentality.

When John and Andrew wanted to sit at Jesus' right hand, his response was "He who would be first must be servant of all." Pastors, evangelists, apostles, prophets, and teachers are not called to be conquerors, but servants. Their role is to equip the saints for the work of ministry and thereby build the kingdom of God. They are not to exploit the laity to build their kingdoms with the biggest church buildings and plush lifestyles. Leaders are to lay down their lives so that the saints or laity may flourish in the work of the Lord so that Jesus may be glorified. There are many fine leaders who do so, but it is time that all the church return to the model Jesus established in the early church, which was patterned after the Jewish model of education.

Jewish influence removed

The paradigm shift that took place after the Roman assimilation of the church into the empire resulted in three major changes:

1. Jews were banned from influence in Roman society. They could not hold public office.
2. The church was stripped of every vestige of its Jewish roots, and a paradigm based on Roman pagan culture was implemented as part of the church infrastructure, substituting idolatry of Mary and the saints as a replacement for Roman gods.
3. The body of Christ was subjugated to a hierarchical system that prohibited evangelism and ministry by non-clerical believers. Instruction in biblical teaching was denied to the laity.

As the Church couldn't be stamped out by three centuries of persecution, beginning in A.D. 317, the Roman Empire found it advantageous to made Christianity the state religion. The Church's Jewish roots were severed in the process. (In Acts 24: 5 and Acts 28: 2, the Church was referred to in Roman circles as being a Jewish sect – "the sect of the Nazarites".) Rome denied the Church its intrinsic "Jewishness", refusing to allow it to continue operating under the original instructional methodology and leadership structure as had been established by the Jewish Messiah and the Jewish apostles. If Rome had not recreated the church in its own image, an indictment would have arisen against the Roman authorities .They would have been forced to admit that a great evil was perpetrated when Roman armies, under the command of Titus and Vespasian, stole the treasures of the temple in Jerusalem, took the riches with them to Rome, destroyed the temple and slaughtered nearly one million Jews in the process. As is the normal scenario with robbery and genocide, the perpetrators sought to justify and cover their crimes. In this case it was done by vilifying the Jews and then stripping the new state religion of all Jewish identity.

The decisions of the First Nicene Council set the stage for centuries of persecution by the Gentile church against the Jewish people. This resulted in much suffering among the Jews inflicted upon them by Christians in the name of Jesus. Many laws, both secular and ecclesiastical, were enacted which brought further oppression on the Jewish people, while the newly redesigned church patterned after the Roman Empire continued to hold firm control over society.

Jews and the Justinian Code

Among those rulings which increased subjugation of the Jews was the Justianian Code. This code of laws was developed from AD 529 to AD 534 under the direction of Justinian I, Emperor of the eastern Roman Empire. The Justinian system of law solidified Christianity as the state religion. It ruled that anyone who was not a Christian was considered a non-citizen of the Roman Empire. This decision made a Jew persona non grata throughout the Empire. Jews were forced to travel from land to land and were unable to enjoy the privileges of citizenship. Some nations of Europe banned Jews from entrance on the principles of the Justinian Code. [6]

Christian Persecution of Jews in the Middle Ages

David Turner, past director of the Jewish National Fund, in a series of blogs on Christian anti-Semitism published in Jerusalem Post, in August 2012, submitted a history of anti-Semitic attacks against Jews by European Christians during the Middle Ages. Turner prefaced his remarks by quoting Irving Borowski who wrote the forward to Fr. Edward Flannery's 1965 book *The Anguish of the Jews*: "one of every two Jews born over the past 2000 years was murdered." Turner points out that previous to A.D. 1000, Jews suffered persecution in the form of Torah burnings and were forced to wear uniformed clothing and badges, as a degradation and humiliation. But after the shift of the first millennium violent persecutions spread throughout Europe:

- A.D. 1009 - Orlean massacre;
- A.D. 1012 - Massacres of Jews took place in Rouen, Limoges and Rome;
- A.D. 1021 – Jews were burned alive in Rome
- A.D. 1063 - Jews were burned alive in Spain;
- A.D. 1065 – the Jews of Lorraine were massacred.

These hideous attacks were followed by an even greater evil: the Crusades. According to Turner, the Crusaders were little more than marauding thieves and murderers who destroyed Jewish villages, confiscated Jewish property and killed Jews across Europe and in the Holy Land (Muslims suffered similar abuse under the Crusaders.), all in the name of Christ.

The Crusades were followed by the Inquisitions of Spain and Portugal where systematic "Christian" persecution and genocide of Jews took place. Jews were forced to convert to Christianity. After their conversion, the *conversos* or newly forced-baptized Jews were scrutinized to see if they still held to any of their Jewish religious beliefs or practices. If there was the slightest suspicion that they might still be Jewish in their hearts, the *conversos* were tortured or, if defiant, they were burned at the stake. Again, this was carried out in the name of Christ and by so-called Christians.

Lateran Councils and the Jews:

The third (AD 1179) and fourth Lateran Councils (AD 1215) held on Lateran Hill at the Vatican focused heavily on the Jews. The following are some of the restrictions and judgments leveled against the Jews by the Church in the third and fourth Lateran Councils: [7]

Jews were required to pay tithes on behalf of any Christian to whom they loaned money. This was so that the church wouldn't suffer loss of money. (There were very few possibilities for Jews to operate businesses in Medieval Europe due to governmental restrictions. The lending of money was one of the few venues available to Jews.)

Jews were forced to wear clothing which distinguished them from Christians. This was done supposedly to prohibit them from having sexual relations with Christian women. (A similar prejudice known as the "Jim Crow" laws in the time of Segregation in the U.S. led to the lynching of many innocent black men who were falsely accused of having illicit relations with white women.)

From Good Friday to Easter Sunday, Jews weren't allowed on the streets or in public places.

Jews were forbidden by the church to hold public offices.

Jews who voluntarily converted to Christianity but held on to any traditions of Judaism were to be forced by coercion or violence to fully comply to the Christian faith.

The last decree of the Lateran Council mentioned provided a carte blanch for the horrific treatment of the Jews in Spain and Portugal during the Inquisition 300 years later. The Lateran Council rulings set a precedent for the evils perpetrated against Jewish people for many centuries to come. It is important to note that these rulings were made by the church, not the state. [8]

Martin Luther and the Jews:

Martin Luther first espoused tolerance for the Jewish people. In a letter to a minister in 1514, Luther wrote that "the conversion of Jews should not be something forced upon them but rather a work of God, converting from the heart, not externally." [9] In 1519, Luther condemned theologians for their hatred of the Jews. And in 1523, Luther wrote a treatise, *That Jesus Christ was born a Jew*, in which he further condemned the ill treatment of Jews by Christians. [10]

However, twenty years later, in 1543, Luther's attitude had taken a 180 degree turn. He wrote a hideous discourse against the Jews called *From the Jews and their Lies* (*Von Juden und Ihren Lügen*) with statements such as:

> The Jews are base, whoring people and no people of God.
>
> Their boast of lineage, circumcision and law must be accounted as filth.
>
> The Jews are full of the devil's feces and they wallow in it like swine.
>
> The synagogue is a defiled bride; yes, an incorrigible whore and an evil slut.
>
> Synagogues and schools should be set on fire, Jewish prayer books destroyed, rabbis forbidden to preach, Jewish homes razed and their money and property confiscated.
>
> They should be shown no mercy or kindness and offered no legal protection.
>
> These poisonous envenomed worms should be drafted into forced labor or expelled for all time.
>
> In this book Luther also wrote: "We are at fault for not slaying them."[11]

It's hard to believe that these are the words of a "Christian" leader and not excerpts from Hitler's book, *Mein Kamp*.[12] Luther's ravings against the Jewish people were an open door for the growth of anti-Semitism in Germany. Through Luther the stage was set for the Holocaust which took place four hundred years later in Germany.

The German Evangelical Church

As Luther set the stage for the Church's complicity and collaboration in the Holocaust, the German Evangelical Church under the leadership of Reich's Bishop Ludwig Müller brought to fulfillment Christian participation in Hitler's abuse of the Jewish people. Müller, as Hitler, sought to establish a "Church of the Reich". Müller wanted a coalition of Catholics who, together with the Protestants, would endorse and propagate the doctrine of National Socialism. Müller developed a Germanic New Testament with an Aryan Jesus. During his time as Bishop, the Old Testament was banned which was also the wish of Hitler.[13]

In 1933, Müller managed to gain approval by the National Socialist government for the establishment of the "German Evangelical Church". The new denomination amalgamated the church, the government of Adolf Hitler and the people of Germany as an entity. Segments of the Baptist and Methodist churches aligned themselves with Hitler, as well. Christian dissenters were silenced by arrest, imprisonment, torture and execution. [14] Many Christians were expelled from Germany.

Photos by permission of Bavarian State Library,
Munich, Germany

Pro-Hitler German Evangelical Christians

Photos by permission of Bavarian State Library,
Munich, Germany

Hitler as god-father to Goebel's baby's baptism, Bishop Müller presiding

Photos by permission of Bavarian State Library,
Munich, Germany

Papal Annuncio Torragrossa with Hitler

Photos by permission of Bavarian State Library,
Munich, Germany

Pope Pius XII celebrating mass in Nazi gathering

Photos by permission of Bavarian State Library,
Munich, Germany

Hitler at wedding with Bishop Muller

The Catholic Church and the Holocaust

There is much controversy concerning Pius XII, who became pope in 1939. The irony regarding Pius XII is that, although he is quoted as having made statements against National Socialism, he was seemingly oblivious to the constant pleas he received requesting help for the Jews. Hitler had taken power in January of 1933. On July 20, 1933, the Vatican under Pius XI as pope, signed a concordant or treaty with Hitler which abolished the Catholic political parties and trade unions which were openly opposing National Socialism. In exchange, the church would be allowed to practice church rites, appoint new clergy, and continue running Catholic schools. The Nazi party later violated much of the treaty by persecuting Jesuits and other Catholic organizations. Much research has been done concerning Pius XII as to whether he was an accomplice to Hitler or a clandestine opponent of National Socialism. The research is inconclusive. However, what is apparent is that the church – both Protestant and Catholic – could have done much more to oppose Hitler. Had both the Catholic and Protestant churches risen up against Hitler and National Socialism as a whole, it is doubtful if the Final Solution would have been realized. [15]

Conclusion:

Through the heretical doctrine of replacement theology which had its beginnings in the schism of the church from its Jewish roots, the church was erroneously taught that God had rejected the Jews. Over the centuries following the First Nicene Council, Jesus' Jewish roots were erased in Christian Europe. Paintings of Jesus in many churches depict a blond-haired, blue-eyed European dying on a cross. The church was reduced to the mentality of the Christian woman in the museum who said to the two Jewish women, "How dare they say Jesus was a Jew?" Persecution and oppression of the Jewish people by Christians became common place, even being justified by the writings of leaders within the church and by church canon. Centuries of persecution against Jews by Christians consummated in a majority of Germany's churches blindly joining forces with the Reichs Church and the National Socialists to become complicit in the atrocities of the Holocaust.

Following the decisions of the Nicene Council and the third and fourth Lateran Councils, Christians initiated pogroms against the Jews, persecuting the very brethren of Jesus. In the Middle ages Jews were slaughtered across Europe under the slanderous label of being "Christ killers" or for the false accusation of blood libel which prompted mob attacks on Jews. The atrocities committed against the Jews of Europe in the name of Christ were numerous.

The church's control over the minds of the people, coupled with the decisions of the First Nicene Council and restrictions on laity regarding Bible study, set the stage for European Christians to become ready abusers of the Jews. Martin Luther's change of heart from toleration to a livid hatred of the Jews influenced future generations in the nation of Germany and elsewhere. Only in this last century, since the Holocaust and the prophetic restoration of the nation of Israel, have Christians begun to awaken and understand the position and importance of the Jews as the chosen people of God. Only now are Christians beginning to understand their God-given mandate to stand with the Jews.

1. Schaff, Phillip: *History of the Christian Church, Vol. II, Ante-Nicene Christianity, A.D. 100-325*). Nabu Press, 2011. (original date of publication, 1923.)

2. Eusebius, *Life of Constantine, Vol. III*, Ch. XVIII, Loeb Classical Library, No. 153, 1926.

3. Theodoret of Cyrus: *Ecclesiastical History*, Ch. 9. Kessinger Publishing, 2010.

4. *The Holy Bible, King James Version.*

5. *The Holy Bible, New American Standard Version.*

6. Kunkel. W.: An introduction to Roman Legal and Constitutional History. Oxford, 1996, pg. 157.

7. Halsall, P. *Fourth Lateran Council, 1215, Canons on the Jews.* Medieval Sourcebook. 1996.

8. Thompson, J.W. & Johnson, E.N. *An Introduction to Medieval Europe, 300-1500.* N.Y., N.Y.: Norton & Co. 1937, pg. 652.

9. *Luther's Correspondence and other Contemporaneous Letters,* trans. Henry P. Smith, Phil. P.A.: Lutheran Publication Society, 1913, pg. 1:29.

10. 1Luther, Martin: *That Jesus Christ was born a Jew.* Trans. W.I. Brandt, in *Luther's Works.* Phil. P.A.: Fortress Press, 1962, pg. 200-201, 229.

11. (Luther, Martin: *On the Jews and Their Lies,* pg. 154, 167, 229. cited in: Michael, Robert: *Holy Hatred: Christianity, Anti-Semitism and the Holocaust.* New York: Palgrave Macmillian, 2006, pg. 113.)

12. Hitler, Adolf: Mein Kamp.

13. Robbins, H.C. The Germanization of the New Testament by Bishop Ludwig Mueller and Bishop Weideman. London, 1938.

14. Barnett, Victoria. For the Soul of the People: Protestant Protest against Hitler. Oxford University Press, 1992, pg. 33.

15. *Reassessing Pope Pius XII's Attitudes toward the Holocaust.* Jerusalem Center for Public Affairs, 2009.

PART TWO

CHAPTER 11

Current Threats against the Jews

Muslim terrorists and jihadists, neo-Nazis and right-wing extremists, and news media such as the BBC, CNN, and *The New York Times* have one thing in common: their opposition to the state of Israel. However subtle or direct this propaganda may be, it has a profound influence on the society in which it is being disseminated. Therefore negative propaganda against Israel being promoted by each of these organizations is having an equally destructive effect. It each case it is working to intensify anti-Semitic sentiment through biased, unbalanced information against Israel among the local population where it is being broadcast or printed.

Israel's enemies are as diverse as are their propaganda tactics. An open-minded observer of the divergent forces affecting public opinion on matters concerning the Middle East (and thereby representing real threats against the Jewish state and the Jewish people) can readily conclude that an all-out misinformation war is in progress. This assault, waged through propaganda and rhetoric, has served as a catalyst to create hatred toward the Jewish people, worldwide.

The predominant sources currently threatening Israel and the Jewish people are: 1) jihadists and Islamic propaganda; 2) neo-Nazi and right-wing extremists; 3) media manipulation of news reports into propaganda against Israel; and 4) popular opinion, or what is called "political correctness." Although these influences differ in their ideological approach toward the Jewish people and Israel, the results are similar. The methodologies and the consequences warrant examination.

CHAPTER 12

Jihadist and Islamic Anti-Zionism and Anti-Semitism

Terror has unfortunately become a common word in today's culture. The incidents are numerous, to mention a few:

The Lockerbie bombing: Libyan terrorists bombed a Pan Am jet over Scotland, killing 270 passengers, crew, and people on the ground in 1988.

The Munich Olympics attack in 1972 in which eleven Israeli athletes and coaches were killed by Arab terrorists. (This operation was funded by Mahmoud Abbas, chairman of Fatah and elected leader of the Palestinians.)

The first intifada, from 1987 to 1993, in which Arabs killed a thousand Palestinians accused of collaboration and 164 Israelis.

The second intifada, from 2000 to 2005, also called the Oslo War, in which 1,100 innocent Israeli citizens died in suicide bombings, car bombings, shootings, and by other means.

The World Trade Center-Pentagon attacks of September 11, 2001, in which nearly three thousand people died.

The Madrid train bombings of 2004 in which 181 died and eighteen hundred were wounded.

The underground bombing in London on July 7, 2005, in which fifty-two were killed (and four of the bombers as well) and more than seven hundred injured.

The bombing of a hotel and the Chabad Center in Mumbai, India, in 2008 in which 164 died and 308 were wounded, including the Rabbi and his wife who ran the Chabad Center.

The killing of three children and a teacher at a Jewish school in Toulouse, France, on March 19, 2012. The gunman, Mohamed Merah, was on a motor scooter and sped off after the attacks. Merah, later killed in a shootout with police, said that he had links to al Qaeda and that the murders were in retaliation for attacks on Palestinian children and the presence of the French army in Afghanistan.

All of these attacks were a result of Islamic terror tactics. But where did Muslim extremists get the idea to commit such atrocities against unarmed, innocent people? How did it all start?

Hitler and the roots of Islamic terror

Few people realize that the Muslim jihadist-terrorist movement has its foundations in the relationship between the Grand Mufti of Jerusalem and Adolf Hitler during World War II. In 1941, Haj Amin al-Husseini, the Grand Mufti of Jerusalem and self-appointed leader of the Arab community in British Palestine, fled to Germany after having instigated riots against the British in Jerusalem. He met with Hitler during his stay in Berlin. The two concurred on the "necessity" of forcing the British out of Palestine. Al-Husseini requested Hitler's help in keeping the Jews from entering Palestine. Hitler assured him that German policy regarding Palestine would give "positive and practical aid to the Arabs."[1] Hitler also reiterated that Germany's objective was "solely the destruction of the Jewish element residing in the Arab sphere."[2]

Photo by permission of Yad Vashem

Grand Mufti with German officers, Nov. 1941

1

דער ירושלימער גרויס מופטי באזוכט די באסנישע ס.ס.
טריוויליקע.,פון דער דייטשישער צייטונג " די פאסט"
פון 9 פעברואר 1944.

Photo by permission of Yad Vashem

The Mufti reviews Muslim SS Troups

The Grand Mufti later aided the German war effort by training twenty thousand Bosnian Muslims as SS troops. After the war, the Mufti, having come under French protection, lived in exile in Egypt and operated a terror network against the new state of Israel from Cairo.

One of his most famous disciples was a young nephew by the name of Yasser Arafat. Arafat later founded Fatah and Hamas, the two terror organizations currently leading the government of the Arabs living in Israel. (Hamas is on the list of US government- recognized terror organizations, whereas Fatah is not. However, Fatah appears on other lists of terror organizations.) The Al Aksa Martyrs Brigade, an offshoot of Fatah and a closely associated organization, has performed what it calls "retaliatory attacks" or acts of terrorism on Israel on a regular basis.

Islamic terror attacks perpetrated today bear a marked similarity to the work of Hitler and his cronies during the early days of their rise to power in Germany. These organizations make verbal threats against the Jews and the West, as Hitler did. They are open about their objectives to destroy Israel and the Jewish people, as was Hitler. Indeed, Hitler's influence through the Mufti has left an indelible mark on the Islamic terror movement. The great irony is that Mahmoud Abbas, the present leader of Palestinian Arabs, wrote a doctoral dissertation at a Moscow university entitled "The other side: The secret relationship between Naziism and Zionism." As absurd as this sounds, Abbas continues to try to deceive people with this ridiculous comparison.

Another lying accusation promoted by Abbas' government is that Israel has created an "apartheid state" similar to South Africa and that Israel is a "racist" government. These fabrications couldn't be further from the truth. As a result of continuous terror attacks against Israeli civilians during the second Intifada, Israel was forced to build the security fence that Abbas uses to justify the accusation of apartheid. For self-protection, Israel constructed a wall down the middle of the country to stop the flood of suicide bombers who were killing Jews on a nearly daily basis. The security fence reduced these attacks and brought an end to much of the terror.

As to the charges of racism, Israel is a land of many nationalities and ethnic groups. Immigrants have come from all parts of Europe, the Arab nations, Ethiopia, China, northern India and South America. Israel is a rainbow of people from all backgrounds. Israel's demography includes Jews, Druze, Maronites, Copts, Bedouins, Samaritans, and immigrants from nearly all nations..

However, as has been said, if you tell a lie long enough, people do begin to believe it. This was true of Hitler and it is certainly true of the propaganda the Palestinian Authority and certain factions within the United Nations have used against Israel. The UN has now held two conferences on racism, with the main aim being to condemn Israel as racist, likening the security wall erected after the second intifada to the apartheid system of South Africa. Nothing could be further from the truth. However, this propaganda has achieved its purpose in creating more poison against Israel. Hitler, Hamas, and Haman have all used slander and lies to carry out their evil agendas. Hell's strategy has not changed in twenty-six hundred years.

1. Mitchell Bard, *The Mufti and the Führer* (Jewish Virtual Library, 2012).

2. Record of conversation between the Führer and the Grand Mufti of Jerusalem on November 11, 1941, in the presence of Reich Foreign Minister and Minister Grobba in Berlin, *Documents on German Foreign Policy, 1918-45, Series d, Vol. XIII* (London: 1964), p. 881f, in Walter Lacquer and Barry Rubin, *The Israel-Arab Reader,* New York: Facts on File, 1984, pp. 79-84.

CHAPTER 13

Neo-Nazi and Right-Wing Extremists

On July 22, 2011, I was standing on a street car platform in Oslo, Norway, when I heard a loud blast that shook the foundation under my feet. I later found out that a single right-wing extremist had bombed and destroyed government buildings in the city. Anders Behring Breivik then went to a nearby island and killed more than seventy young people representing the youth movement of the Labor Party.

In 1997, I was taking an escalator up to the second floor of the train station in Hamburg, Germany. On the descending side of the escalator, a man gave the "Heil Hitler" salute to a man standing on the stairs behind me. This man returned the salute.

On a visit to Munich, I encountered a gang of skinheads with swastika symbols on their leather jackets. They were running through the streets and angrily shouting and pushing people. In Schwerin, Germany, I saw a similar gang of skinheads, although they were not demonstrating.

On European television, I have seen frequent reports concerning violent acts perpetrated by neo-Nazis and white extremist groups.

White extremists, or white nationalists, and neo-Nazis are not benign groups of misfits and malcontents, isolated from society in small-town Germany or Idaho. The neo-Nazi movement and closely associated right-wing extremist and militia groups have a dangerous agenda that must be made known.

Common beliefs and objectives

White supremacists (groups such as the Ku Klux Klan and Arian Nation) and neo-Nazis (those adhering to the ideology of Adolf Hitler) share much in common. They believe that whites are superior to all other races. Therefore, any group that would supplant the white race must be eliminated or suppressed. Extremist groups tend to be militant and are often armed, adding to the danger they present.

Among the values held by these groups is an elitist intolerance which promotes the suppression of all other races to advance the white race. Ultra-nationalism, seen in European countries, seeks to elevate ethnic Europeans above other races and cultures. The extremists also call for the expulsion of other ethnic groups living in their countries, such as Jews, Muslims, and Gypsies.

Those unacquainted with the activities of neo-Nazi and white extremist groups may well see their impact as being isolated and less serious than it is. A review of news reports concerning their activities provides a better understanding of the danger such groups pose.

There are indications that nationalist groups are growing in number and membership throughout Europe. An article headlined "Human rights under pressure," appearing on February 15, 2012, in the Norwegian newspaper *Aftenposten*, reported: "There is a danger of neo-nationalism over the whole European continent. We know from history that with the spread of neo-nationalism attacks on minorities and increased racism follows." [1]

These hate groups attack and kill minorities. Very little is being done to stop the groups or to place surveillance on them. Extremist groups seem to be successful in spreading their doctrine of hatred if unchecked.

Neo-Nazi activities and attacks

- Jerusalem Post, May 8, 2012: **Extremism in Europe**. Both the far right and far left parties in France made strong showings in recent elections and pose a threat to France's Jews from both sides. The left which received 15% of the vote are collaborating with Islamists and may become a part of Hollande's coalition. The right – Le Pen's party - is a nationalist party, considered by some French people to be quasi-Nazi in their ideology.

- In the London mayoral election, a virulent anti-Semite, Ken Livingston, narrowly lost to the incumbent with 48% of the vote. Livingstone has condoned suicide bombers in Israel and calls Israel an apartheid state.

- Greece's Jewish Community is faced with growing voter support of the Golden Dawn neo-Nazi party which received 7% of the vote in June while Syriza, an anti-Zionist, anti-Israel leftist party came in 2nd with 29% of the vote.

- In the Jerusalem Post, April 14, 2012, the headline read: "American Nazi Party has registered its first lobbyist in Washington, D.C. [2]

Der Spiegel, a widely circulated German magazine, wrote in its January 2, 2012, issue: "There is scarcely a week that goes by in which a politician or government official isn't attacked by neo-Nazis." The article said that neo-Nazis smash windows of cars, homes, and offices of left-wing politicians. They have been known to cut the cables for brakes on cars and to make anonymous death threats against leftist ministers. [3]

The Canadian Broadcasting Corporation released a video from January 5, 2012, showing a neo-Nazi group in Vancouver beating a black man.

In 2009, the London *Daily Mail* published a report on an attack by masked neo-Nazis at the former Matthausen concentration camp in Austria. A group of elderly camp survivors had gathered to commemorate the Holocaust victims who had died at that camp. Neo-Nazis first attacked a group of ten Italian survivors with shouts of "Heil Hitler" and "This way to the gas chambers." They then focused on a group of fifteen elderly French former camp inmates and shot plastic bullets at them, wounding one in the neck and one in the head. One of those present managed to pull the mask off of one of the neo-Nazis and snap a photo of the assailant with a cell phone. The perpetrators spoke a local dialect. [4]

On November 17, 2011, *Zaman Today,* a Turkish-English newspaper, reported that neo-Nazis had killed eight Turkish immigrants and one Greek immigrant.The report implied that the murderers may have had connections to German officials. [5]

The Independent, a London newspaper, in an article dated November 14, 2011, reported the arrest of a gang member in the killing of eight Turkish kebab stall owners. This gang, the National Socialist Underground, was also linked to a bomb blast in Dusseldorf in which several Russian Jewish immigrants were hurt. [6]

On November 9, 2011, Russian television reported that neo-Nazis attacked Ukraine World War II veterans commemorating victory over Hitler. The report said that such groups were becoming more militant in other former Soviet states, such as Estonia, Lithuania, and Latvia.

On July 26, 2011, *The Local,* an English-language paper in Germany, reported an arson attack on a house where Roma, or Gypsy, people were living. The attack took place near Cologne, Germany, four days after the white supremacist Anders Behring Breivik attacked Norwegian government buildings and killed seventy-six people in Norway. [7]

The Washington Examiner, in an article dated August 11, 2011, reported that Aryan Nation member Buford Furrows was found guilty of the murder of a Filipino-American postal worker and five counts of attempted murder at a Los Angeles Jewish community center in 1999. [8]

On March 28, 2010, Norway's *Aftenposten* reported on the growth
of neo-Nazi and anti-Jewish groups throughout Europe. The
article mentioned an attack on twenty-two-year-old Shalom
Dov Ber Halem while the young Jewish man was riding a
bicycle in Holland. An Orthodox rabbi in Amsterdam, Raphael
Evers, reported that anti-Semitic attacks were getting worse and
more frequent in Holland with each passing year. Evers was
dismayed that the people of Amsterdam were no longer shocked
by these episodes. Evers said he suffered harassment every time
he left his house. Bloeme Evers-Emden, an eighty-five-year-
old Dutch survivor of Auschwitz, said that anti-Semitism and
attacks on Jews in Europe were much worse than they were
before World War II. [9]

Aftenposten on May 16, 2010, reported the election of neo-Nazis to
the parliament in Hungary. Fascists are winning elections to key
government positions in many nations of Europe. [10]

Aftenposten's front-page headline of March 28, 2010, read: "More
violence and hate against Europe's Jews." Under the picture of
a desecrated Jewish cemetery, the article reported: "Fear and
anxiety spread throughout the Jewish communities of Europe.
Jewish children are bullied in school, adults are beaten up, and
synagogues and Jewish cemeteries are being desecrated. Over all
of Europe, there is an alarming rise in anti-Semitic attacks." [11]

On April 15, 2009, *Aftenposten* published a picture of Jews in Berlin
entering a synagogue covered with SS symbols and anti-Jewish
slogans. The vandalism followed the arson attack on a Jewish
kindergarten on March 1, 2007. [12]

This is just a minute review of current events pointing to the rise
of anti-Semitism and the growth and activity of neo-Nazi and white
supremacist groups in recent years. Unfortunately, the problem is of

a much larger scale than these few reports indicate. All fair-minded people must maintain awareness and speak out against this injustice. As Christians, we must take this as a call to stand with the Jewish people in the midst of rising anti-Semitism.

1. *Aftenposten*: *Human rights under pressure,* Feb. 15, 2012.
2. *Jerusalem Post, "American Nazi Party has registered its first lobbyist in Washington, D.C.",* Ap. 14, 2012.
3. *Der Spiegel,* Jan. 2, 2012.
4. *Daily Mail, Neo-Nazis attack concentration camp survivors,* May 12, 2009.
5. *Zaman Today, Neo-Nazis kill immigrants,* Nov. 17, 2011.
6. *The Independent,* Nov. 14, 2011.
7. *The Local,* July 26, 2011.
8. *The Washington Examiner,* Aug. 11, 2011.
9. *Aftenposten,* Mar. 28, 2010.
10. *Ibid,* May 16, 2010.
11. *Ibid,* Mar. 28, 2010.
12. *Ibid,* Ap. 15, 2009

Chapter 14

Media Propagandizing against Israel

The world's media are waging a PR war against the Jewish state. This campaign of slander and manipulation of the news is working not only against Israel. Such propaganda also fosters anti-Semitism and further attacks on Jewish people in the nations where these reports are being published.

There is an apparent consensus among news media that reports concerning the Middle East should be slanted against the Jewish state. From European media to CNN, NPR, and other television, radio, and newspaper sources, coverage of the Middle East seems to be intentionally distorted, filled with half-truths, or lacking of information that would lead to fair and balanced reporting. For example, if Israel, having been hit by missiles coming out of Gaza, has counterattacked, the media report would read something like this: "Israeli defense forces bombed a house in Gaza, killing two."

What is omitted here? It has been conveniently forgotten that the bombing of the house in Gaza was in retaliation for rockets that destroyed Israeli homes or may have killed or injured Israeli citizens. Israel was on the defensive, not the offensive. But the media portrayed Israel as the provocateur on the offensive. A key fact concerning one such incident is that the terrorists who launched rockets on the Israeli town of Sderot did so from the house later hit by Israeli bombs. Those killed in the retaliation were the terrorists who had launched missiles in the first place.

Here are some headlines from September 2011 to March 2012 from *Dag Bladet*, a leading Norwegian newspaper. These reports are examples of slanted reporting and media bias against Israel: [1]

"Jonas Gahr Støre brags on the Palestinians," September 19, 2011. Støre is the Norwegian foreign minister. Jonas Gahr Støre has great influence in Norway and his overwhelming approval of the Palestinians against the Israelis holds great weight with the Norwegian people.

"Will this girl get her own land?," September 21, 2011. A picture of an Arab girl in her mother's arms at a demonstration in Ramallah plays on the emotions of viewers. This coverage neglects the fact that Israel was reborn out of a tragedy that cost over six million innocent Jews their lives and that the land of Israel is the traditional Jewish homeland.

"We are the last occupied land," September 23, 2011. Sympathy only for the Arabs. Not a word about the Jewish side of the story and the fact that the area the Arabs call "occupied" is the biblical area of Judea-Samaria.

"Israeli warship on its way to Palestinian convoy," November 4, 2011. The headline fails to convey that the ship was being sent to search for weapons being smuggled into Gaza from Syria or Iran.

"Israeli air attack on Gaza," November 14, 2011. The headline doesn't mention that the attack was provoked by an Arab attack on southern Israel.

"USA: Israel must develop a better relationship with neighboring nations," December 3, 2011. This headline is taken from a statement by the Obama White House. It shows the prejudice of the leftist American government and the eagerness of European media to use such statements for more condemnation of Israel. It also omits the fact that Israel has been willing to negotiate but Hamas which rules Gaza has declared that it will "never" recognize the nation of Israel as a legitimate state.

"Palestinians killed in Israeli air attack," December 7, 2011. The headline fails to mention that those killed were terrorists who had been firing missiles at Israeli towns.

"The UN asks for billions in aid to Gaza and the West Bank," January 17, 2012. No mention of the needs of Israel, which stands alone in its battle for survival. Untold millions of dollars have already been poured into the Palestinian Authority in the form of humanitarian aid. However, little of the money is used for its intended purpose and is rather used to line the pockets of Fatah and Hamas politicians.

"Hamas moves its leadership from Syria to Gaza," February 6, 2012. Norway has recognized Hamas, which is on the US terror list, as a viable political party and partner for negotiations. This despite the fact that Hamas has declared in its charter that it will never recognize Israel's right to exist.

"Four killed in Israeli attack on Gaza," March 9, 2012. Again, no mention of the fact that the attacks were in retaliation for rockets fired on Israel.

Norway is just one nation. But if these reports serve as representative of current trends in anti-Semitic Europe, it is certainly indicative of an acceleration of the hatred and prejudice with which Europe's Jews are being forced to live.

However, headlines concerning Israel which leave out important truths are not exclusive to European press. The *New York Times* in an article dated June 18, 2012, wrote, *Militants attack workers at border with Egypt, killing one.* [2] A report on the same incident in *The Jerusalem Post* read *Terrorists attack workers at border, killing one.* [3] Why is it that the reports vary in their description of the facts? Why were the so-called "militants" who attacked unarmed Israeli workers not described as "terrorists". The use of the word "militants" is somehow a legitimization of their actions. It softens the fact that an innocent, unarmed worker was killed as others were attacked. Another question this report poses regards the fact that the terrorists were attacking the workers with anti-tank missiles as they were building a security wall. Why didn't the

New York Times object to these **terrorists** possessing such powerful weapons and why wasn't the question asked, "Where did they get the weapons?" Again, we see media downplaying the important questions around the incident. The report in the New York Times seems to seek to legitimize the radical-Islamo-Fascist perspective as being somehow justified, in that "militants" not "terrorists" were attacking unarmed men. The manipulation is very subtle, but clearly evident, none the less. ²

As is easily understood by glancing at these headlines, all of this information is arranged to propagandize against Israel. Some headlines conveniently omit any reference to missiles launched from Gaza that provoked Israeli counterattacks. But one must ask, "What government in its right mind would not strike back against an unprovoked attack by a neighboring entity launching rockets against its cities and population?" Wouldn't Canada strike back against America if the US bombed cities north of the border? Wouldn't France strike back if Germany launched a missile against her? But it appears that in the eyes of the world that there is one nation that doesn't have the right to defend its citizens: Israel.

This barrage of lying accusations against Israel is bad enough in itself, but it has another ramification that often goes unnoticed. Such media manipulation results in the growth and intensification of anti-Semitism against Jews living in those nations where the news distortions are broadcast.

To gain a clear perspective on the media propaganda to which Israel is subjected, it is necessary to analyze media coverage of the Jewish state. In the beginning of the new millennium, as a volunteer on behalf of the Israeli Embassy in Oslo, I took official translations of articles from Norwegian newspapers, provided by Leif Røssak, then the embassy's information officer, to media in New York City. These reports showed how the news media manipulated the facts to create propaganda against Israel. Eventually the reports did receive media attention in the US. Unfortunately, nothing has changed and the media continue to unfairly represent Israel.

Media awareness

The following brief review of Norwegian press reports discusses the influence of media manipulation against Israel on the Norwegian public.

Gabi Gleichmann, a Swedish Jewish journalist, wrote in an article for Norway's *Aftenposten* on April 15, 2009: "Europe's Jews live with fear and threats. Nine years ago (2000) delegates from 45 countries met in Stockholm to discuss the Holocaust and pledged to fight anti-Semitism in a more determined way. The year after (2001,) fire bombs were thrown into synagogues and Jewish schools in France and Belgium. Jews were attacked openly on the street. This happened without the authorities in these countries seeming to pay any attention. France's Chief Rabbi, Joseph Sitruk, advised the people in his synagogue to avoid wearing any Jewish religious symbols on the street. But this didn't help. The anti-Jewish hate and attacks have grown in number and intensity year by year. Philosopher Shmuel Trigano has proposed the question as to whether it is at all possible for Jews to live in France." [4]

Henriette Jevnesveen, a student at Oslo University studying for her master's degree in religious history, surveyed students at a youth club in Oslo. The response, reported in *Aftenposten* on June 17, 2011, was shocking. "'I have nothing against Jews, but I wouldn't want any Jews to come here.' This wasn't an unusual response to the question about Jews. The students were open about the use of 'Jew' as a negative word ... My findings show that having a different religious affiliation wasn't important as to how the youths would choose their friends. But one group was not represented in the club, youth of Jewish lineage ... One of my informers says that she would not like Jews to move into that area. 'It wouldn't be good.' According to this student, a possible interpretation as to why Jews don't fit in with other youth is that Jews would create an unbalanced society. If people with a recognizable Jewish identity should move into the district, those living there would be forced to take a stronger stand on their viewpoint concerning hatred of Jews." Jevnesveen said that the youths who expressed the strongest hatred of Jews refused to be interviewed. She said that they clearly understood that their views were considered negative. Jevnesveen said the most aggressively anti-Semitic youths were in control of the others. They set the standards for acceptance in the group by their hatred. The more passive members of the youth club were complicit in this virulent anti-Semitism. Asked what the source of these prejudices was, the club leaders said it was a result of the situation in the Middle East. But the attacks are focused on local Jewish youth. This Jew-hatred is coming from the next generation of leaders in Norwegian society. But in France, where anti-Semitism has been researched in depth over the past few years, the results showed that there wasn't necessarily a correlation between events in Israel and anti-Semitism. Some of the youths questioned said that hatred of Jews came from theories that everything having to do with them is less worthwhile and that Jews hold world power. Are "The Protocols of the Elders of Zion" being revisited? [5]

Responding to a survey of adults in Norway, published in *Aftenposten* on November 28, 2008, Hilde Henriksen Waage, a professor in Middle Eastern research at Oslo University, said that anti-Semitism was not a growing problem in Norway and that the problem was Israel and Israel's policies. However, four other people interviewed, including a bishop, another leader in the Lutheran state church, the general-secretary of the Norwegian press corps, and Shoaib Sultan, general-secretary of the Islamic Council of Norway, all agreed that anti-Semitism was a growing problem. The bishop, the state church leader, and the press corps general-secretary felt that news coverage concerning Israel contributed significantly to the anti-Semitism, while Sultan and Professor Waage felt media coverage of the Middle East was fair and balanced. [6]

Dr. May Lund, a medical doctor and professor of medicine in Oslo, maintains that there is a direct correlation between anti-Semitism in Norway and the prejudicial and unbalanced criticism of Israel in the media. She cited a study by ten European countries (Denmark, the Netherlands, Belgium, France, Germany, Austria, Switzerland, Italy, Spain, and England). The study conducted a survey to find out if there was a direct correlation between anti-Semitism and anti-Israel sentiment. The results showed that those with the most prejudice and strongest hatred of Jews had an equal level of dislike and prejudice against Israel. [7]

Manfred Gerstenfeld, director of the Jerusalem Center for Public Affairs, in his book on Norwegian anti-Semitism, *Norway, behind the humanitarian mask,* accuses Norway of being an important producer of anti-Jewish and anti-Israel sentiment. He says that Norway's news coverage is pro-Palestinian and that Norwegian academicians and politicians tend to be anti-Semitic and anti-Israel. Jewish children in Norwegian schools are being harassed as well. Gerstenfeld also mentions Norwegians Mads Gilbert and Erik Fosse, whom he says helped to finance Hamas in the last Gaza war. Gerstenfeld said that the heads of Norway's government ignore Arab war crimes and say nothing about Hamas' hatred of Jews and unprovoked rocket attacks on Israel. He says that post-modernist culture in Norway blames Israel entirely for the conflict in the Middle East while closing its eyes to the hate culture being brought into Norway by Muslim immigrants. [8]

Anti-Semitism and hatred of Israel are indeed on the rise in Europe and in the world. On Aug. 2, 2012, Jerusalem Post reported on a speech given by Achmedinijad, Iran's president, in which he declared that the ultimate goal of world forces must be to annihilate the nation of Israel. This type of rhetoric is what Israel lives with on a continual basis.

> The *Jerusalem Post* in an article dated June 13, 2012, wrote: Norwegian student in Oslo burns Jewish pupil. The article reports that a Norwegian student took a coin that had been heated in a grill and placed it on the back of a Jewish student. This student had endured much harassment by his colleagues simply because his father is Israeli. The Simon Wiesenthal Center had investigated the matter and report that the school, the police and the government have given almost no response to the attack which is reminiscent of Nazi-collaborating Norway. [9]

Such media distortion of the facts is not exclusive to European press. Reports on CNN, NPR radio, the New York Times and other media often serve to present a one-sided anti-Israel perspective on the news. This is evident in the above-mentioned report from the New York Times. It has been said that all that is required for evil to prevail is for good men to do nothing. If anti-Semitic speech and attacks are allowed to continue unchecked, western culture will again become susceptible to anarchy and tyranny such as prevailed under Hitler. It is imperative that a strong and verbal opposition to anti-Semitism is rendered by all those who are enlightened. We cannot be silent at a time like this with an ever-growing presence of hatred toward the Jewish people.

1. *Dag Bladet, Nov. 2011-Mar. 2012*
2. Kershner, Isabel: *New York Times.* *"Militants attack Israeli workers at border with Egypt."* June, 2012.
3. *Jerusalem Post, "Terrorists attack workers at border, killing one."* June 18, 2012.
4. Gleichmann, Gabi: *Aftenposten, Europe's Jews live with fear and threats.* Ap. 15, 2009.
5. Jevnesveen, Henriette: *Ibid,* June 17, 2011.
6. *Ibid,* Nov. 28, 2008.
7. *Ibid,,* Ap. 7, 2010.
8. Gerstenfeld, Manfred: *Ibid,* Ap. 2010.
9. Weinthal, Benjamin: *Jerusalem Post:* *"Norwegian student in Oslo burns Jewish Student".* 6.13.12.

CHAPTER 15

Political Correctness and Popular Opinion

I recently heard a phrase on television that struck me as being a profound observation: "There is a militant secularization taking place in the United States." From my personal observations, having lived in Europe for seventeen years at the time of this writing, I can safely say that this secularization has been eroding the Judeo-Christian foundations of European culture for decades. A majority of Europeans find the concept of God and Christian faith to be absurd. It is unacceptable to speak of Christianity in European circles. The European Parliament in Brussels even wrote a constitution for the nations of the European Union that totally negates centuries of Judeo-Christian cultural influence.

Throughout the European nations and now, it seems, in American society, it is not politically correct to speak of one's Christian faith or values. It can cost a person brave enough to do so his social status and his job. This is the fruit of political correctness, the result of militant secularism. Our rights of freedom of thought, religion, and speech are being eroded.

But political correctness has not only influenced the right of Christians to speak out for their faith. As previously mentioned, social attitudes toward Israel and the Jews have also taken on a distinctly negative, prejudicial tone. This is reflected in attitudinal changes of non-Jewish students who attack Jewish children. The use of the name

Jew as a negative word by youths in the school systems of Europe is another alarming trend.

In social gatherings and work situations, discussions of Israel have become points of conflict for those who would defend the Jewish state, making it difficult to express opinions that go against the popular tide.

Socialist political correctness is a standard being imposed on the public by the news media. This trend is spreading throughout society. Socialist-oriented media are re-enforcing a code of beliefs which is being used to direct societal responses. Thus the public is losing the ability to think for itself and to exercise freedom of speech.

Article 30 of the Hamas charter calls for "writers, educators, media people and all those in a position of authority to use their influence on behalf of the Islamic Resistance Movement." It appears that the world's media are complying with this Hamas demand. [1]

In Islamic countries, it is forbidden to speak against Islam, at peril of death. But now in the West, it appears that governments and media are blindly bowing to pressure from Islamo-fascists who would impose the same control over public opinion and freedom of speech.

The implications of this trend are frightening. The same ideological approach was used in Germany after Hitler's rise to power in 1933. There was only one acceptable way to think. There was only one acceptable way to talk. There was a people-the Jews- who were chosen to be hated and made into scapegoats. This hatred united the German people against a common enemy, the minority – the Jewish people. To succeed in that society, it was necessary to agree with the required mind-set and to follow the politically correct trends in both speech and action.

The world must wake up and see that the same strategy is being implemented against the Jewish people by media, politicians, and Islamo-fascists. God forbid that we should continue in this direction. We must learn from the lessons of history or we are destined to repeat an earlier tragedy.

1. *Hamas Covenant,* Yale University, Lillian Goldman Library, 1988.

CHAPTER 16

Transformation: From a Goat Herd to a Sheepfold

Much of the rising tide of anti-Semitism in the world today is being fueled by antagonism against Israel. Islamists are threatening the lives of Jews, while neo-Nazis and white extremists spouting Hitler's hateful diatribes are growing in number. One government after another among the world's nations is turning its back on the little country of Israel. Iran's leaders are determined to destroy her, as are many of the nations surrounding Israel.

According to Romans 11, gentile believers in the Messiah, Jesus, are grafted into Israel as a branch is grafted into a tree. Its welfare is our welfare. We are indeed called to be God's Esther for such a time as this.

But what can we do to combat this menacing wave of hatred and apathy toward the Jewish people and the Jewish state? First, we must allow the Lord to purify our hearts so that they are prepared for His purposes. Second, we need to enter into intercession for Israel. Every move of God is birthed through prayer. Third, it is important that we are informed in order to pray effectively and to act accordingly. Staying informed by following the events and the news reports regarding matters relevant to Israel is an important part of being effective in prayer if we are to counteract anti-Semitism and anti-Israel propaganda. Fourth, we need to find the mind of the Lord concerning the work He would have us to do, as individuals, or as part of an established program focused on supporting Israel and the Jewish people. Lastly, we need to go forward in the work of the Lord, remembering that our warfare is mighty through God.

Do I harbor anti-Semitism in my heart?

It is incumbent upon each of us to search our hearts for anti-Semitic attitudes. These can be in the form of blatant antagonism toward the Jewish people, jealousy, or belief in subtle prejudices and stereotypes. Much of the hate that created pogroms through history was related to stereotypes and lying accusations against the Jewish people. Whether we embrace accusations that Jews killed Jesus or that "all Jews are greedy," we need to go before the Lord and allow Him to rid our hearts of every prejudice and lie that we have believed regarding the Jewish people. If there is sin in our hearts related to envy or jealousy against the Jews, may the Lord show us and deliver us.

Prayer, an essential key

It is imperative that we understand that our fight is not with the visible world. We are warring against demonic forces that have sought the annihilation of the Jewish people for millennia. No amount of money or educational resources would be sufficient to combat the strongholds in the hearts and minds of those who are locked into the prejudice, jealousy, and hatred represented by anti-Semitism. It is necessary that we take our fight to another level.

> The weapons of our warfare are not of the flesh, but divinely powerful for the destruction of fortresses. We are destroying speculations and every lofty thing raised up against the knowledge of God, and we are taking every thought captive to the obedience of Christ."
> —2 Cor. 10:4-5 [1]

Every initiative we undertake regarding Israel and the Jewish people must begin with prayer. And certainly, concerning our stand with the Jewish people and the nation of Israel, it is a necessity to understand the spiritual forces we are opposing. As we pray and seek God, He will reveal how we should wage war and pray effectively.

Daniel's intercession for the nation of Israel, through fasting, is an excellent example of directive prayer under the power of the Holy Spirit. In the 9th chapter of the book of Daniel, Daniel interceded for his people in a prayer of repentance after reading Jeremiah's prophesy which foretold that the people of Israel would be in exile for 70 years. As he read, Daniel realized that the 70 years of captivity was nearly at an end. The angel, Gabriel, appeared to Daniel as he sought the Lord and instructed him on the timing of the coming of the Messiah. Then in the 10th chapter of Daniel after his priestly intercession and repentance for the sins of his people, Daniel again fasted and prayed – this time for 21 days – 3 weeks. At the end of the three week period, an angel was sent in response to Daniel's prayers. This angel told Daniel that he had been dispatched from the beginning of the time when Daniel had first begun to fast and pray. The angel further explained that the prince of Persia, no doubt a demonic ruler spirit over the nation of present day Iran, had hindered the angel from coming to Daniel. Michael, Israel's national guardian, had joined the angel in the fight against the demon rulers over Persia which made it possible for the angel to come to Daniel. He thereby delivered the message of the end times in response to Daniel's 21 day fast. This fascinating history is revealing as to the intricate nature and importance of fasting and prayer.

In the sixth chapter of Ephesians, Paul further elaborates on intercession and warfare as he explains that our warfare is not against human beings but against principalities, powers of darkness, spiritual wickedness in high places and the rulers of the present darkness – a satanic hierarchy. Fasting and prayer is a powerful means of breaking through demonic resistance in the second heaven.

Another important tool in intercession for Israel is found in Jesus' instruction regarding binding and loosing. Jesus said that he has given us power to tread on serpents and scorpions and all the works of the enemy so that they will in no way harm us. (Luke 10:19) This is not referring to snakes and bugs but rather to demonic powers. Jesus also said that if we are going to plunder the enemy's fortresses or strongholds, we have to first bind the "strong man" or ruler spirit. (Matt. 12:29 and Mark 3:27) Jesus further explained to his disciples that they had authority that whatever they bind on earth will be bound in heaven and whatever they loose on earth will be loosed in heaven. (Mark 16:19 and Mark 18:18) This authority is ours, in the name of Jesus. There is no formula for using the weapons of intercession. Effective intercession is prayer under the directive of the Holy Spirit. The gateway for the supernatural workings of the Holy Spirit is through prayer in tongues. As we pray in tongues and wait on the Lord he will show us how to wield the sword of the spirit and how we can take down demonic powers over our nation, our families, our lives and on behalf of the nation of Israel.

There have been times when the Lord has awakened me in the night to pray against terrorism. He has shown me specific places to pray about and how to pray. Within a few days, I have heard of terrorists who have been arrested and their missions aborted in the cities to which I had been directed in my prayer time. I am sure many others were praying, too. But it is exciting to be an intercessor and to see God validate the results of prayer on the news.

This holds true in the area of intercession for Israel. However, rest assured that God knows the enemies of His people, Israel, and that if you and I will pray and intercede for Israel's well-being, God will show us specifically what to pray about. You may see the results in the newspaper a few days later!

Intercession for ourselves is important if we are to know what God would have us do for Israel. As we fast and pray, God may lay on our hearts a specific work particular to us or He may call us to be part of an established work. We must also be aware that there will be opposition to His plan. We must overcome every stronghold and plan of the enemy that would hinder us from our calling. Perseverance is a necessity. It may take fasting and prayer. It may take an investment in travel, time, money, and energy. But whatever the Lord calls us to, He will give us all we need to accomplish it. It is important that we be faithful and see it through, just as Esther did when she fasted and prayed and took the action God had assigned her.

I have been an intercessor for Israel for many decades. While active as a professional singer living in New York, I often sang for Zionist organizations in the United States and then later in Europe. One day on a bus going up Madison Avenue to my home in Washington Heights, the Holy Spirit came on me and I began to pray in the Spirit and weep silently. This went on for about a half-hour. Then my mind was filled with poems about our friends in Washington Heights who had survived concentration camps. One by one, I wrote the first drafts that became the song cycle *Voices of the Holocaust*[2]. The vignettes, or spoken monologues that tell their stories from the camps, came on a flight from Paris to New York City in the summer of 2005.

The song cycle that Marilee Eckert and I composed (she did the major work of composition) has been performed in New York City, where it premiered in 1997 with more than one hundred Holocaust survivors present among the audience of approximately three hundred. It was then performed in Oslo at the Edvard Munch Museum auditorium. Helsinki came next in 2005, with members of the Helsinki Philharmonic and Finland's Musician of the Year, Juhani Aaltonen, joining us on stage. Tallinn, Estonia, was the next venue, with a first performance in the National Cathedral. At this concert, an Estonian pastor asked forgiveness for the sins of the Estonian people against the Jewish people. (Hitler's forces didn't have to kill the Jews of Estonia; the Estonians did it for him.) Two days later, the work was performed at the Jewish School of Tallinn with Rabbi Shmuel Kot present. This was one week before the opening of the first synagogue in Tallinn since World War II. (The original synagogue was destroyed by the Germans during the war). When we initially approached Rabbi Kot about presenting a Holocaust concert in Tallinn, he said, "This is big. This is God. We will do everything we can to help you help us." The song cycle *Voices of the Holocaust* with monologues, has since been presented in Holocaust memorial concerts in France, Berlin, Germany, and Latvia.

In 1994, I attended four performances of Beethoven's *Fidelio* at the Metropolitan Opera in New York City within two weeks. I didn't know why I was compelled to see the same opera repeatedly. (*Fidelio* is the story of the liberation of a political prison is Spain.) But as I sat viewing my third performance, I began to pray in the Holy Spirit. I then had a vision of the stage transformed with a totally different set—not a political prison in Spain in the 1700s, but Auschwitz in 1945. I saw on the stage before me the arch at the entrance of Auschwitz, which carries the German text *Arbeit macht frei* (Work makes for freedom). I saw the opera characters dressed in Nazi uniforms or wearing the striped costumes given to prisoners at Auschwitz. I saw the commandant who liberated the prison dressed as Eisenhower when he entered Dachau.

I went home and wrote up my ideas. A friend, Wendy Bortoli, who had been an artist for the Pentagon, made drawings from my ideas. But it wasn't until sixteen years later that the concept was finally mounted. Opera is expensive but funding was provided. *Fidelio: A Holocaust Memorial Production*[3] was executed in the opera houses of five major Polish cities. The orchestra, soloists, chorus, and conductor were among Poland's finest. We had an internationally acclaimed stage director from the Israeli opera.

However, *Fidelio: A Holocaust Memorial Opera* was one of the fiercest battles we had ever fought. As a matter of fact, we came close to giving up. But God wouldn't let us and He gave the victory. The production received an excellent review in the world's leading opera magazine. All of this was a result of prayer - not just our own prayers, but that of dear prayer warriors who backed up the production. Prayer is the key to all work for the Lord and all work for Israel and the Jewish people.

Fidelio Holocaust Opera:
Krakow, Poland

Another breakthrough that resulted from prayer was the establishment of International Voice of Justice, a non-profit organization dedicated to Holocaust education through music and the arts. This organization became a reality in 2009. IVOJ has now produced events in many countries of Europe.

It is essential that we seek the Lord and find out what He would have us to do. Only then can we have peace to pursue the decisions we face in life and work for the kingdom, and stand with Israel. Fervent, effectual prayer does avail much.

Be informed

To be effective in intercession, we need information regarding threats against Israel, about her internal and external problems, and about threats against Jews living in the Diaspora. Many Web sites are helpful to this end. *The Jerusalem Post* and *Haaretz,* two leading Israeli newspapers, are a good place to start.

Following the local news and trying to discern whether reports are fair or slanted can be quite important. Calling local news media when they distort reports on Israel is a good idea. This lets them know that there are observers who are aware of their propaganda.

A good source of information about anti-Semitic attacks and related developments is the Simon Wiesenthal Center website, which offers news coverage of anti-Semitism worldwide. These reports appeared on the site in February of 2012: [4]

February 5: A German pastor denied the legitimacy of the Jewish people.

February 6: The Wiesenthal Center requested that the European Parliament investigate Swedish broadcasting's anti-Semitic discourse.

February 6: The Iranian appeal to destroy the Jewish people is unparalleled since Nazi Germany.

February 9: A US Marine unit in Afghanistan used a flag with the Nazi *SS* on it as the symbol of the unit.

February 9: The Presbyterian Church of the USA has a recent extensive history of anti-Semitism. Under pressure, the church removed its Israel-Palestinian Facebook page, which frequently printed anti-Semitic propaganda, such as inferences that the White House is controlled by Jewish lobbyist groups.

February 14: Apple's iTunes app, which functions as a thesaurus, provided classic stereotypes when the word *Jew* was searched for synonyms. Among the words that came up were *stingy, miser,* and *mangy.*

February 16: Paris University plans a "Cancel Israel Apartheid" conference. This presents a threat to public order and a danger to the Jewish community of France.

February 17: An anti-Semitic attack on a Venezuelan opposition leader was reported.

February 20: Activists within the Presbyterian Church demand that the church divest from Caterpillar, HP, and Motorola, three companies that "profit" from business in Israel.

February 20: A neo-Nazi march is held in Kovno, Lithuania.

February 21: An Anti-Defamation League poll shows that 15 percent of Americans are anti-Semitic. Since the meltdown of the euro currency, anti-Semitism in Spain stands at 74 percent; in Hungary, 76 percent; in France, 33 percent; in Poland, 36 percent; in Russia, 34 percent; and in the United Kingdom, 15 percent.

February 26: Venezuela seeks a position on the United Nations Human Rights Commission, an unconscionable request given Hugo Chávez's record on anti-Semitism and his suppression of opposition and dissidents. (Chavez has been host to Achmedinajad of Iran and is favorable to Iran and Al Quida.)

These reports offer a world view from twenty days of observation. It is alarming to see how widespread the reports are. And it is tragic to learn that Christian organizations are a source of anti-Semitism, as well. (Jerusalem Post, Aug. 16, 2012, reported that The United Church of Canada, that country's largest Protestant denomination, voted to boycott Israeli products from the settlements in the West Bank and East Jerusalem. These areas are the Biblical areas of Judea and Samaria.) A plumb line has been drawn regarding Christian sentiment toward Israel and the Biblical right of the Jewish people to the land. Christians are faced with a choice today. We are going to have to choose the truth of the word of God to Jacob whose name was changed by God to Israel: "The land I gave to Abraham and Isaac, I also give to you and to your descendents after you." Let God's word be true and every man a liar, but His word shall prevail over popular opinion and political correctness. He is the God of Israel!

Seek God concerning His plan for your life

God's call to the church is "Comfort ye my people. Speak ye comfortably to Jerusalem." God's mandate for the Church toward Israel is more important now than it has ever been. Jewish people have begun to take notice that Christians are speaking out on behalf of Israel. Prime Minister Benyamin Netanyahu said in a Christmas greeting to the world's Christians in December 2011, "Israel is proud of its strong and growing Christian community and we are proud of the deep and passionate support of so many Christian friends of Israel around the world."

It has been a great privilege to know and minister along side Jan Willem van der Hoeven. To my knowledge, Jan Willem is the finest speaker concerning matters related to Israel in the Christian world. He established the Christian Embassy in Jerusalem some years ago when many nations' embassies were moved from Jerusalem to Tel Aviv. He is now the director of the International Christian Zionist Center in Jerusalem. Jan Willem is one of the pioneers in this field, and his impassioned preaching and love for the Jewish people have served as a major catalyst in the church's awakening to the importance of the Jewish people in God's plan.

A staunch supporter of Israel was Kaare Kristiansen. Kaare was a member of parliament and former head of the Christian Democratic Party in Norway. I first met Kaare when Haakon and I performed a concert for the Norwegian Prime Minister and heads of state. Kaare later served on the Nobel Peace Prize Committee. When the committee decided to give the Peace Prize to Yasser Arafat in 1994, Kaare Kristiansen resigned in protest. He was strongly criticized in the Norwegian press for his opposition to the choice of Arafat for the prize. Haakon and I read about Kaare's courage in the New York Times before we returned to Europe. When we came to Norway we read about the rejection and criticism Kaare was experiencing in the Norwegian press, Haakon and I decided to prepare a concert to honor Kaare. Working with a team of Norwegian Christians, the concert was arranged. It was also decided that a petition supporting Israel and demanding that Norway stop pushing Israel to give up land, should be circulated among Christians and then be presented to the parliament. When Kaare addressed the public at the concert he admonished everyone to take a strong stand for Israel and against those who were trying to pressure Israel to give up land. The concert was followed by a march through the streets of Oslo with Israeli flags. Three members of the parliament supporting our action met us at the house of parliament and received the petition. We had invited over 100 pastors of churches in Oslo to join us. Only three pastors would participate. Many of the pastors of the churches openly admitted that they thought it was "too controversial" and they wouldn't risk involvement. (This is a tragic scenario in the city which was the source of the Oslo Accords, a so called peace treaty which forced Israel to give up much land with little or no guarantee of peace or concessions on the other side. The Oslo Accords eventually led to the 2nd Intifada.) The concert and march took place on the firth anniversary of the signing of the Oslo Accords, a fact that we were not aware of until the actual day of the event. The concert was a success and the church was filled with Christian supporters of Israel, in spite of the church leaders who didn't want to get involved. Kaare Kristiansen was a great man and set a standard of uncompromising excellence. It was a privilege to be able to honor this great man as we began our European work in support of Israel.

Margaretha Jægerhult, director of Operation Lifeline in Helsinki, Finland, is another champion for Israel. Margaretha, a widow, has traveled the world helping Jews make *Aliyah,* or immigration to Israel. Her work has spread throughout the former Soviet Union, China, North Africa, Europe, the United States, the Carribean and Central America. She has helped Jews from many nations return to Israel. In

Russia, China, the Caribbean, and Europe, Margaretha, an ordained minister, has instructed Gentile Christians on God's eternal covenant with the Jewish people.

The Rev. John Hagee, senior pastor of Cornerstone Church in Texas, is active in arranging events to honor Israel throughout the United States. He holds a summer conference in Washington, D.C. that brings many thousands of Christians together to lobby Congress in support of Israel.

Each of these servants of the Lord has had an impact on the church, bringing understanding and empathy for the cause of Israel and the Jewish people. All of them have paid a price in prayer and in giving their time to accomplish God's plan. Israel needs each one of us to be galvanized on their behalf.

Israel's glorious future

God has promised Israel and her people a hope and a future. As Jeremiah wrote: *"I know the plans I have for you. Plans for good and not for evil to give you a future and a hope. Then you will call upon Me and come and pray to Me, and I will listen to you. You will seek Me and find Me when you seek Me with all your heart. I will be found of you, declares the Lord, and I will restore your fortunes and will gather you from all the nations and from all the places where I have driven you." Declares the Lord, "and I will bring you back to the place where I sent you into exile."* (Jer. 29:11-14, NAS)

God has promised the Jewish people that He will restore His relationship with them as he restores them to the land of Israel.

> *"I will set my eyes on them (the captives of Judah) for good, and I will bring them again to this land; and I will build them up and not overthrow them, and I will plant them and not pluck them up. I will give them a heart to know me, for I am the Lord; and they will be my people and I will be their God, for they will return to Me with their whole heart.* Jer. 24:6-7, NAS

The re-establishment of the nation of Israel has set the stage for a day prophesied by many prophets when Israel will be surrounded by armies. Jesus will appear with the host of heaven and destroy the nations that would seek to destroy Israel. In that day, all Israel will see Him. Zechariah who saw that day prophesied:

> *"In that day the Lord will defend the inhabitants of Jerusalem, and the one who is feeble among them in that day will be like David, and the house of David will be like God, like the angel of the Lord before them. And in that day I will set about to destroy all the nations that come against Jerusalem. I will pour out on the house of David and on the inhabitants of Jerusalem, the Spirit of grace and of supplication, so that they will look on Me whom they have pierced; and they will mourn for Him, as one mourns for an only son, and they will weep bitterly over Him like the bitter weeping over a firstborn.* Zech. 12:8-10, NAS.

The God of Israel will, indeed restore His people to their promised land and deliver them. He has promised, also, that he will dwell in Jerusalem.

> *"I will return to Zion and **will dwell in the midst of Jerusalem**. Then Jerusalem will be called the City of Truth, and the mountain of the Lord of Hosts will be called the Holy Mountain. Zech. 8:3, NAS.*

God has promised that the Jewish people will return to the land from the nations where they have been scattered.

> *"Then I Myself will gather the remnant of My flock out of all the countries where I have driven them and bring them back to their pasture, and they will be fruitful and multiply. As the Lord lives, who brought up and led back the descendants of the household of Israel from the north land and from all the countries where I had driven them. Then they will live on their own soil. Jer. 23:3, 8 NAS.*

> *"Lift up your eyes round about and see; they all gather together, they come to you. Your sons will come from afar, and your daughters will*

be carried in the arms. Then you will see and be radiant, and your heart will thrill and rejoice." Is. 60: 4, 5. NAS

We have seen this prophesy fulfilled since the reestablishment of the nation of Israel in 1948 when Jews returned from all nations, out of the inferno of the Holocaust to the nation of Israel. Although many came to the land in poverty, resources were provided and the land was rebuilt.

Amazingly, God promised that He would restore the nation of Israel in one day:

"Who has heard of such a thing? Can a land be born in one day? Can a nation be brought forth all at once? As soon as Zion travailed, she also brought forth her sons." Is. 66: 8, NAS

Israel was birthed in one day when the United Nations voted to reestablish a Jewish State on May 14, 1948. No other nation in history has been established in an instant as Israel was. Rather, peoples have emerged as nations as a result of centuries of development.

God promised that when the Jewish people would return to their land, the desert would blossom and bear fruit:

"Indeed, the Lord will comfort Zion; He will comfort all her waste places. And her wilderness He will make like Eden, and her desert like the garden of the Lord." Is. 51: 3, NAS

"The desert will rejoice and blossom." Is. 35: 1, NAS

Anyone who has traveled through the nation of Israel can see the amazing agricultural developments which have come about since 1948. Previously Israel was an arid desert. Now it supplies a major portion of the fruits and vegetables consumed in Europe and elsewhere.

God has promised to restore his relationship with the Jewish people.

"At that time," declares the Lord, "I will be the God of all the families of Israel, and they shall be my people." Thus says the Lord, "The people who survived the sword found grace in the wilderness-Israel, when it went to find its rest." The Lord appeared to him from afar saying, "I have loved you with an everlasting love; therefore I have drawn you with loving kindness. Again I will build you and you will be rebuilt, O virgin of Israel! Again you will take up your tambourines, and go forth to the dances of the merrymakers. Again you will plant vineyards on the hills of Samaria; The planters will plant and will enjoy them. . . Behold I am bringing them from the north country, and I will gather them from the remote parts of the earth, among them the blind and the lame, the woman with child and she who is in labor with child, together, a great company, they will return here, with weeping they will come, and by supplication I will lead them; I will make them walk by streams of waters, on a straight path in which they will not stumble; for I am a father in Israel."

. . . Hear the word of the Lord, O nations, and declare in the coastlands afar off, and say, "He who scattered Israel will gather him and keep him as a shepherd keeps his flock." For the Lord has ransomed Jacob and redeemed him from the hand of him who was stronger than he. They will come and shout for joy on the height of Zion, and they will be radiant over the bounty of the Lord-over the grain and the new wine and the oil. They will return from the land of the enemy. There is hope for your future," declares the Lord, "and your children will return to their own territory." Jer. 31:1-5, 8-12, 17-18.

Israel has a bright future according to the promises of God, even if her current situation is one of peril.

Your voice is important

God wants to use you as an "Esther for such a time as this." Israel needs your voice.

Proverbs 31:8-9 New American Standard Bible: Open your mouth for the mute, for the rights of all the unfortunate. Open your mouth, judge righteously and defend the rights of the afflicted and needy. [5]

Proverbs 31:8-9 King James Version: Open your mouth for the dumb (those who cannot speak) in the cause of all such as are appointed to destruction. Open your mouth, judge righteously and plead the cause of the poor and needy. [6]

Proverbs 31:8-9 Amplified Bible: Open your mouth for the dumb (those unable to speak for themselves). For the rights of all who are left desolate and defenseless. Open your mouth, judge righteously, and administer justice for the poor and needy. [7]

The world is increasingly aligned against Israel. The Jewish people in the Diaspora face growing threats to their welfare. The world's media is often biased in their reporting, which promotes anti-Semitism. The Jewish people and the Jewish state are surrounded by enemies on every side. Jews of the Diaspora face neo-Nazis, Islamo-fascists, biased media, antagonistic public opinion, and growing anti-Semitism in schools and in the streets of Europe and other parts of the world. The church must rise up and speak out! If the church of Germany had spoken out against Hitler and taken a stand as the church of Denmark did, perhaps there would not have been a Holocaust. Israel needs us now!

It is important that we are bold and uncompromising. If we don't stand for Israel, who will? As Christians, we should know and understand God's covenant with the Jewish people. The Jewish people have a right to the land that God gave to their fathers, Abraham, Isaac, and Jacob. God's covenant with them is eternal. It will never change.

We must not be silent as were the majority of Christians in Europe during the Second World War. Nor should we be like those who embraced stereo types and prejudices against Jewish people which led them to carry out anti-Semitic pogroms over the centuries. Members of the resistance who saved Jewish lives had a choice before them, and that same choice is ours. We may face rejection and opposition, but the rewards far out-weigh the costs. We may even find that our opponents will have their eyes opened as we stand for truth.

A former colleague began to rant against Israel and came out with some alarming anti-Semitic rhetoric. This man was a college professor. I recognized his words as *politically correct* jargon which circulates among those seeking to sound sophisticated and liberal. It was shocking to hear him spouting such unfair antagonism against Israel. I was compelled to take a stand which led to some tense moments between us. But I am grateful to report that he has now become friends with Jewish people and is more moderate toward Israel.

We must oppose unfair criticism of Israel. We must oppose media that distorts reports on Israel. We must oppose anti-Semitism in every possible way. We must oppose it with truth and with our talents and abilities. If you can write, write the truth about Israel. If you can sing, sing the songs of Zion. Whatever your talents, Israel needs your help now more than ever before. If you are an intercessor, pray in the Spirit and pray with knowledge.

With the record of abuses committed by the church over the centuries, it is imperative that those of us who know the Messiah and understand the importance of Israel in God's plan do all we can to counteract burgeoning hatred toward the Jews. But how can we do that?

The church has been given a mandate in this prophetic season. Our eyes have been opened. We know the eternal importance of Israel and the Jewish people to God. We have seen through the lies and propaganda propagated against the Jews and the Jewish state. We understand that news broadcasts are being slanted and that hatred of the Jewish people is rising. But what should be our response?

Proverbs 31:8–9 gives us a clear mandate on where to begin in the war against anti-Semitism. We are commanded to open our mouths for those who can't speak for themselves, those who are appointed for destruction. We are to fight for the rights of those who are desolate and defenseless. We are to administer justice and judge righteously.

In January of 2012, a memorial was held in Berlin to commemorate the Wannsee conference of 1942. At this secret meeting 70 years before, fifteen Nazi officials designed the Final Solution. The fate of more than six million Jewish people was decided in Wannsee which led to the Holocaust.

At the 2012 commemoration, leaders of the German and Israeli governments, Holocaust survivors, leaders of the Jewish community of Berlin, and evangelical Christians met to remember the tragic events that followed the Wannsee Conference of 1942. The gathering was led by German evangelical Christian, Harold Eckert, director of Christians for Israel, and Tomas Sandell, leader of the European Coalition for Israel, based in Finland. Through this conference, a coalition of Christian leaders throughout Europe was formed, to work together with the Ministry for the Aged in the Israeli government, to raise funds to improve the quality of life for Holocaust survivors in Israel. Many survivors live far below the poverty level. This act demonstrated the love of God to the Israeli leaders and the Jewish community of Berlin in attendance more than anything the Christians of Germany could have done.

God desires to use us to help Israel and the Jewish people. Let us seek Him and allow Him to show us what He would have us do.

The judgment of God on the nations will be based on what they did or didn't do concerning Israel. Those nations judged righteous in their treatment of the Jewish people will be blessed by the Lord. Nations can change. But change begins with the decision of each individual to stand up for truth, no matter what that may cost. If we speak out and don't compromise, we can change our nation. It is important to remember Jesus' words concerning the treatment of the Jews: "Inasmuch as you have done it unto the least of these, my brethren, you have done it unto me."

1. *The Holy Bible, New American Standard Version.*
2. Smith, Martha: *Voices of the Holocaust, A musical drama.* Text: Martha Smith,
3. Music: Marilee Eckert and Martha Smith. 1995. Copyright: Library of Congress.
4. Smith, Martha: *Fidelio: A Holocaust Memorial Production,* copyright 1994, Library of Congress.
5. Simon Wiesenthal Center, *News,* www.wiesenthal.com.
6. *The Holy Bible,* American Standard Version.
7. *The Holy Bible,* King James Version.
8. *The Holy Bible,* Amplified Version.

Lightning Source UK Ltd.
Milton Keynes UK
UKOW041322021212

203042UK00002B/55/P